Britannia

Icon on the Coin

Britannia

Icon on the Coin

Katharine Eustace

Series edited by Kevin Clancy
A Royal Mint Museum publication

First published in Great Britain in 2016
Published by the Royal Mint Museum
Llantrisant, Pontyclun CF72 8YT United Kingdom

www.royalmintmuseum.org.uk

Text © Katharine Eustace 2016

ISBN 978-1-869917-02-9

A CIP catalogue record for this book is available from the British Library

Designed by Tuch, London

Printed in the United Kingdom by Gavin Martin Colournet Ltd, London

. . . .

Front cover Penny of Edward VIII, 1937,
C. W. Coombes. Bronze (detail). RMM50.

Frontispiece Halfpenny of Charles II, 1672,
John Roettiers. Copper (enlarged). RMM719.

The
Royal
Mint
MUSEUM

Foreword

Sir Roy Strong

The figure of Britannia first entered my consciousness in any significant way in 1956 when, as a postgraduate student of the late Dame Frances Yates, I was put to work on Lord Mayor's Pageants. There I came across Anthony Munday's *The Triumphes of Re-United Britannia* (1605), a pyrotechnic of antiquarian learning celebrating the accession of James VI of Scotland as James I of England, thus re-creating the island as a whole as it had been first ruled over by the mythical Trojan Brutus. At the same time I came across a back view of Britannia herself in a frontispiece to a major work by John Dee, *General and Rare Memorials* (1577), where the lady is imploring Elizabeth I, enthroned in a ship, to create a mighty empire based upon maritime endeavour.

Then there was the antiquarian William Camden's *Britannia* anticipating in its title the demise of great Gloriana and the arrival of James I. Here, for the first time, at the top of the title page, we see the Britannia of the second century Roman coins resurrected as an icon for the country and nation. Some 60 years on this two dimensional record of a Roman coin was to migrate from the page to find a three dimensional reality in the coinage of Charles II, who cast himself as Neptune presiding over a watery empire. It is the story of the descent of this image across the centuries on our coinage which Katharine Eustace tells, one which rises and falls with the fortunes of the nation. In today's terms it is wildly politically incorrect, an image asserting the country's imperial maritime dominion over most of the globe. But for centuries it embodied the heroic and triumphant security of an island kingdom whose members could with pride sing, as they still do each *Last Night of the Proms*, 'Rule Britannia, Britannia rules the waves'.

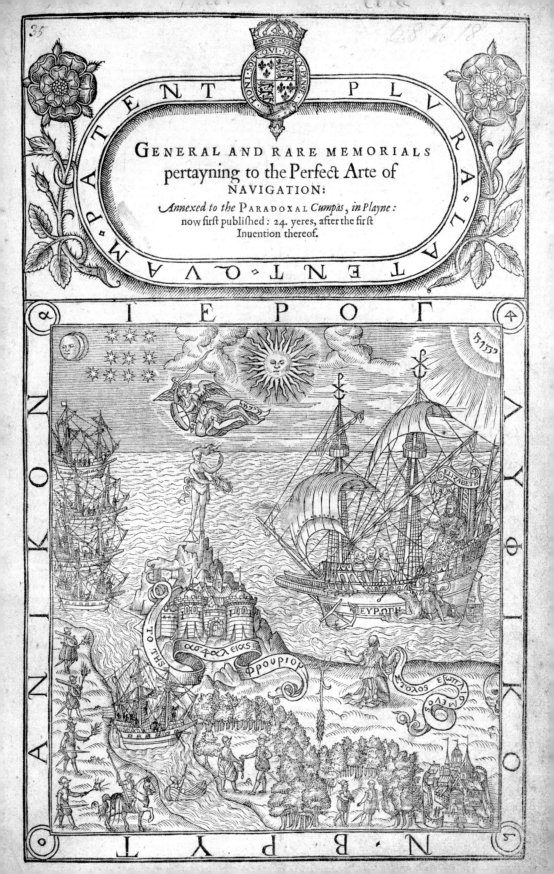

GENERAL AND RARE MEMORIALS
pertayning to the Perfect Arte of
NAVIGATION:
Annexed to the PARADOXAL *Cumpas, in Playne :*
now first published : 24. yeres, after the first
Inuention thereof.

Chapter 1
Βρεταννία:
a collection of islands

Opposite Relief from the Sebasteion, Aphrodisias, first century AD. Marble. Sebasteion-Sevgi Gönül Gallery, Aphrodisias, Turkey.

A high relief of a naked soldier, wielding a sword over the head of a fallen Amazon, was excavated in 1980 at the archaeological site of Aphrodisias in south-west Turkey. The damaged marble panels celebrate the Emperor Claudius' victory in Britain. The inscription on the Britain relief, *Tiberios Klaudios Kaisar / Bretannia* ('Tiberius Claudius Emperor / Britannia'), itself a rare survival, tells us what we need to know: as the artist Scottie Wilson once put it, 'It's all writ out for you'. Stylistically this is a skilfully imitative Roman example of the generic Hellenistic type commemorating battles against the legendary Amazons. It appears to be unique, and, having been found so recently,[1] has no bearing on the long history of Britannia on the British coinage. It does, however, provide an illustration for the argument that so often surrounds any change to the images used on coinage. The existence of this unfamiliar image of Britannia was brought to the attention of a wider public at the time of the complete redesign of the coinage in 2008, when the classicist Mary Beard referred to it in her regular on-line column, *'A Don's Life'*.[2] Nevertheless, after more than 300 years, the 2008 issue did not retain Britannia on the reverse of any of the new coins, though she remained in circulation on the 50 pence piece.[3]

Icon on the Coin is an exploration of the record of this most powerful and successful of national symbols, taking the coinage as the main impulse, and the most consistent manifestation of this phenomenon.[4] It looks for the source and inspiration for the image of Britannia, who has appeared on the reverse of the lowest common denominations of British coinage from 1672 to decimalisation in 1971. It considers the historical context and the political, social, economic, technological and artistic factors that influenced what change there has been to the image. Britannia on the coinage is one of the most enduring of secular symbols, and one of the most stable in terms of design.

Britannia on the coinage has not, in herself, been a subject for deep research,[5] nor indeed until recently has the symbol of Britannia in the wider field. Look up Britannia in the index of any work of history or art history and references are practically non-existent, except incidentally to illustrations making some other point.[6] This has been the case despite her significance as a concept, and her rich visual expression at certain moments in the history of Britain.[7] But things change,[8] and when in 2004 the *Oxford Dictionary of National Biography* was published, it included, for the first time, an entry on the fictive persona of Britannia.[9] Since then there has been a marked increase in interest in Britannia and what she represents.[10]

This entirely symbolic character has lent her name to innumerable activities and developments across the 300 years since she was first formally adopted on the coinage. Associated as she was from the earliest days with the sea and seafaring, there have been generations of ships named for her, from the first *Britannia* launched in 1682. In 1769 there was a *Britannia* in the Hull Whaling Fleet owned by Sir Samuel Standidge Berry, while a West Indiaman *Britannia* was painted by the Bristolian artist Joseph Walter in 1838.[11] In the 1880s the first of the Cunard Line, a paddle steamer with sails, was named *Britannia*.[12] A royal racing yacht in the 1930s was superseded in 1953 by the official royal 'yacht', styled HMY *Britannia*.[13] On 10 March 2014 Her Majesty the Queen named the largest cruise ship ever built *Britannia*, while the Britannia Royal Naval College, Dartmouth, reiterates its historical link with the monarchy. This connection with the sea, and its commercial and social significance, has been repeatedly underscored in the design for the coinage.

From the beginning Britannia's name was associated with reassurance and confidence. The earliest evidence of this was the introduction of a compulsory silver standard in 1697,[14] known as the Britannia standard, as a deterrent against sterling silver coinage being used to make domestic silverware.[15] At the other end of the metallic scale there was 'Britannia' metal, a type of pewter with a high proportion of tin, often used for electroplating with silver for luxury goods for the middle market in the mid nineteenth century. Britannia's name was further appropriated by industry in the nineteenth century, for example, in the Britannia Ironworks, Bedford, which specialised in agricultural equipment, and Andrew Handyside's Britannia Ironworks in Derby which supplied every sort of manufactured iron from colliery equipment to fountains.[16] Britannia was associated with engineering achievements in the great age of British engineering, structurally in the design by Robert Stephenson for the Tubular or Britannia Bridge over the Menai Straits, completed in 1850. In twentieth-century transport, her name was given to the Britannia Class steam engine built in

Below The West Indiaman *Britannia*, 1838. Joseph Walter. Oil on canvas. National Maritime Museum, London. BHC2351.

the Locomotive Works at Crewe in 1951, and to the Bristol Britannia turboprop aircraft made by the Bristol Aeroplane Company. When introduced in 1957 it was a Britannia that made the first non-stop flight to New York.

In popular culture Britannia has been associated with hotels, inns and pubs which boast of patriotic food and drink, of beer and cider, fish and chips, and bangers and mash. Most of the traditional signs for pubs are painted versions of the Britannia on the coinage, and rarely does the borrowed image differ from the composition on those first coins wherever it appears. In commerce and trades her name lends an air of reliability and trustworthiness, as in building societies, insurance and mortgage companies; in trades such as building and plumbing, driving schools, removal companies; and in innumerable advertisements.

Britannia has been successfully exported as an instantly recognisable type, often accompanied by a lion, and absorbed into other cultures as in the image of *Bharat Mata*, or Mother India, most obviously in popular, brilliantly coloured poster, street or 'bazaar' art.[17] In India, a country deeply affected by the meaning of the image of Britannia as Empire, these subliminal appearances may appeal to, even seek out, the implied stability of this image, particularly in the mid 1960s when India was at war with Pakistan.

The unfashionable status of Britannia in the post-war years, coinciding as it has with the long reign of Queen Elizabeth II, may have been largely due to intellectual and cultural embarrassment at the end of Empire. Latterly she has acquired a curious, anti-establishment fashion as in 'Fool Britannia' in 1960s satire, New Labour's 'Cool Britannia' in the arts in the late 1990s, 'Punk Britannia' in popular music, and exhibitions and displays devoted to 'Rude Britannia' and 'Queer Britannia', laden in varying degrees with irony.[18]

Above Insurance company sign, 1730. Lead. Museum of London. NN15880b.

Below *Six British Paralympic Athletes*, 2004. John Lessore. Oil on canvas. National Portrait Gallery, London. NPG 6669.

FOOL BRITANNIA

PETER SELLERS JOAN COLLINS ANTHONY NEWLEY

written and devised by

LESLIE BRICUSSE & ANTHONY NEWLEY

CEL 902

ember

The Sunday Times Magazine

AUGUST 19 2012

THE BEAUTIFUL GAMES

A Spectrum celebration
LONDON 2012
in glorious photographs

LAURA TROTT
OLYMPIC CHAMPION
CYCLING

A Stick of Rock

RUDE BRITANNIA
BRITISH COMIC ART

STYLE

OF THE SUNDAY TIMES

20 MAY 2012

THE MIDLIFE CLUBBERS
DANCING, DEBAUCHERY AND STILL IN BED BY MIDNIGHT

INTIMIDATED, MOI?
AA GILL ON CLEVER WOMEN AND CLEVER FOOD

RULE
BRITANNIA
BRING ON THE PAGEANT, PUT OUT THE BUNTING

IT'S A GOLDEN AGE OF

BRITISH DESIGN

The connection with the anthem 'Rule Britannia' is obvious. In John Lessore's group portrait *Six British Paralympic Athletes*, unveiled at the National Portrait Gallery in June 2004, the references to a popular Britannia are unmistakable.[19] As Empire recedes into the past, so Britannia becomes a legitimate area of retrospective interest and research, to be looked at anew.

Owning dies for coins has, historically, equalled power, the residual implications of which in the early twenty-first century are reflected in contemporary anxiety about national sovereignty, the euro and the dollar. The business of production is an aspect which in all epochs and civilisations most affects attempts at producing a sound currency which is both proof against counterfeiting and instantly recognisable.

One of the refrains throughout this long history is the practical one of style of manufacture and the technology of making coins. Until the technological revolution of the past quarter century the process of design has been long and slow. It is a complex process to change the designs on coinage, to agree a design, to transfer it to plaster models as much as ten inches in diameter. By a reduction process the image is then transferred to the block of steel that forms the die.[20] This hard-won technique has in recent years been accomplished by computerisation which has made this intricate translation process altogether easier and quicker. However, the making of the dies themselves remains a highly skilled art, a late emanation in mass production of the lost art of engraving.[21] So there is, or has been, an inherent reluctance to change, which is enhanced by the more abstract need for stability, and the conservativeness of the providers and users of coins. Indeed, the barely perceptible rate of change, while intensely observed and recorded with scholarly assiduity by distinguished numismatists such as Charles Wilson Peck, may explain the paucity of research into the design and development of the image of Britannia as she appears on the coinage.

Technical considerations must always affect the nature of design, as these in turn affect the choice of raw materials and their sources, questions of intrinsic value, and the constant vigilance needed against fakers and forgers. Metallurgy in its finest form is the business of coining, so that dies of the fittest steel can be proved, and the ingredients of copper and latterly nickel alloys are tried and tested for the best results. This has most recently been reflected in the introduction of bimetallic coins, itself a defence against the counterfeiter. Then there is modern machinery. Changes in design and in the look of Britannia, the 'type', have often occurred with the introduction of technical innovation. Both of these are the stuff of numismatics. Computerisation has affected the process of design and the different stages of production. Although coin production has not been the work of one or two men tapping away at dies with a hammer for a very long time, nevertheless the industrialisation of the Mint was a slow business. The Royal Mint has had its headquarters at Llantrisant in South Wales since moving from Tower Hill, a process begun in 1967 in anticipation of the change to a decimalised coinage. The new Mint is itself the result of the economic and social needs of a developing region in the late twentieth century. It is now a highly successful industrial complex on an impressive scale, supplying coinage for numerous countries around the world.[22]

Opposite Montage of Britannia references in post-war culture: *Fool Britannia*, 1960s satire; *Rude Britannia*, Tate Britain, 2010; Cool Britannia revived for London 2012 Olympic Games; Traditional pub sign, Richmond upon Thames.

Sometimes inherent technical problems may affect design. For example, Britannia has rarely appeared just as a head on the reverse of a British coin. This is largely because the coinage of these islands has almost always carried the head of the monarch on the obverse, hence the expression 'heads or tails?'. Even during the Commonwealth in the mid seventeenth century, after the use of initial shield ornament on both sides, Oliver Cromwell's profile appeared on the obverse on the late coinage of the interregnum, itself indicative of shifts in power. Technically heads on both sides of the same coin had, until recently, been unsound, often causing 'ghosting' or 'shadows' where, under the pressure of the strike, the metal is drawn from one or other side.[23] Thus it was rarely attempted, although a recent exception is the high denominations of gold bullion coins by Philip Nathan and Suzie Zamit, where the thickness of the metal and relatively small production runs have allowed for heads-and-heads. In France the obverse is not already bespoke for a portrait, as no single Frenchman, not even a president, is above the rest. The French emblem, 'Marianne', can appear as a head, and indeed as a portrait.

The French have proudly used as instruments of state the portraits of famous women on their coins, banknotes and stamps. The model for Rodin's *La France* in 1907 was the English actress and artist's model who went by the stage name Julia or Juliette Benson.[24] In more recent times the film stars Brigitte Bardot (1969) and Catherine Deneuve (1985)[25] have posed for portraits of the fictive Marianne,[26] the national symbol of liberty. In 1999 36,000 mayors across France voted for Laetitia Casta, the woman they felt most represented the spirit of Marianne, while in 2013 Inna Shevchenko, an asylum seeker from Ukraine, was chosen for a new stamp. In marked contrast, Britannia on the coin has rarely been a known portrait, the most notable exception being the very first, in 1672, where the evidence points to the sitter as Frances Stuart, Duchess of Richmond. Queen Victoria herself may have inspired the work of members of the Wyon dynasty in the mid nineteenth century, and a daughter of a Chancellor of the Exchequer stood for Britannia at the end of Victoria's reign and the beginning of Edward VII's. Ironically the anonymity of the models for Britannia may have contributed to that static sense of continuity that has been such an important part of her long hold on the collective psyche of the nation.

The consistently bland quality of Britannia's features, which for the technical reasons already described have not been much used in close-up, lends itself specifically to anonymity; indeed her companion the lion has often had more personality. The authoritative figure is thus raised above the personal and speculative, while never being in competition with the likeness of the reigning monarch on the other side of the coin. This is particularly significant when the monarch is a woman, which has been the case for almost half of the 300 years under review. If the anonymity is 'blown', then inquisitive journalism takes over, as happened when the Royal Mail decided Britannia would adorn a £10 stamp, which, issued in 1993, was the most expensive stamp of the day. It became the subject of a curiously well-informed, and at times funny, and always facetious article by the novelist Julian Barnes entitled 'Real Britannia' in the *New Yorker* magazine in the April of that year. Two years later published as a collection of essays, the title was pepped up as 'Britannia's New Bra Size'.[27]

The lack of personality has allowed for an inevitable and useful ambivalence between the dual roles inherited by Britannia from her classical forebear Pallas Athene, who incidentally, according to Greek myth, built the first ship; or in her Roman translation Minerva and her alter ego Roma. One of these roles is as goddess of war, as protector and defender of the state. An early example of this is a medal struck in 1694, in which Minerva threatens a kneeling Louis XIV with a Medusa-masked shield.[28] The other is as goddess of wisdom and peace, as the promoter and encourager of education and culture. The presentation of either of these roles and their attributes, given period style, are almost and conveniently identical and interchangeable.

Another leitmotif concerns style. The prevailing style of Britannia has been Classical, taking its cue from Greece and Rome, whether Mannerist, Augustan, Neo-Classical or Greek Revival. Even Modernism can be seen to defer to the Classical. Western Europe's fascination with the Classical world has amounted to an obsession since the sixteenth century, a fascination which has expressed itself visually over and over again in architecture, painting and sculpture. In its own era Rome was deferential to the Classical world of Greece, and at the margins of the late Roman Empire usurping emperors looked back three centuries for literary and visual sources for their coins. An acute deference to the Classical past emerged at the end of the Gothic age, with the fragmentation of the pan-European world of Christianity, itself centred on Rome. This went hand-in-hand with Humanism and later with the Enlightenment, the birth of the nation state and the search for culturally-identifying roots in the past. Against a pattern of increasing and accelerating change, Britannia remained a safe and superficially static, but steadfast, image across 300 years. What follows concerns the endurance of that image, the image of Britannia.

Above **Marianne de la Jeunesse** stamps depicting Inna Shevchenko as Marianne, 2013. David Kawena and Olivier Ciappa. © Getty Images.

Below **The Bombardment of the French Coast**, medal, 1694. Christian Wermuth. Silver (enlarged). British Museum, London. 1885,0406.2.

Chapter 2
A passion to command it

The figure of Britannia first appears on Roman coins for brief moments in the second and third centuries, when emperors were personally engaged in making history in these islands. Britain was Tacitus' 'war-like province',[1] and the sheer volume of coins struck reflects a continuing need for currency in an area of the Empire that required three legions to hold it down, compared to the one legion needed in North Africa.

Legionaries were paid about one *denarius* a day, and were Roman citizens while non-citizens served as auxiliary troops, and slaves were not allowed to enlist.[2] All were given land, money or citizenship on retirement, and encouraged to settle and to intermarry wherever they had been garrisoned. The Emperor Septimius Severus increased military pay and, according to the historian Cassius Dio, on his deathbed advised his sons Caracalla and Geta to 'enrich the soldiers and ignore everyone else'.[3] So coin was certainly needed. This policy had established many lively military centres such as the legionary fortresses at Caerleon, Chester and York. Its success brought with it the importation of Roman ways, and trade in goods from all over the Empire, such as olive oil and wine from the Mediterranean, glass from the eastern Mediterranean via Trier in Germany, and fine red Samian-ware pottery, produced mainly in France. This would solidify the *Pax Romana* in Britain for almost 400 years.

Personifications of other places and nations had appeared already on the coinage of the Emperor Trajan. The idea of a territory, tribe or province personified as a woman was applied to subjugated nations as imperial Roman expansion was consolidated, the design perhaps specifically adapted for the coin in which the provincial garrisons were paid. Thus Gallia, Dacia, Africa and so on usually appear in feminine form as the personification of territories under Roman dominion, their individual identity heightened by the realistic detail of their native dress.[4] Their names are often inscribed in the exergue.

The earliest types of Britannia on the coinage appeared under the Emperor Hadrian, the first appearing on the reverse of a copper *as* struck in Rome in about AD 119, on which Britannia nonchalantly sits, legs akimbo, on a rocky outcrop or possibly a wall, looking outwards, the exergue beneath her inscribed BRITANNIA. Following the strong strand of realism in Roman aesthetics at the time this early personification of a province is particularised by tribal or barbarian costume: Britannia wears a short tunic, *braccae* or breeches,[5] short boots and a fringed cloak fastened on the right shoulder, flowing over her upper left arm and shoulder, and swathed behind to come back to cover her knees. She holds a spear in the crook of her left arm which rests on a shield, the boss of which is sometimes spiked. Of the provincial types that were to follow representing other regions in the Empire, only Britannia had a spiked shield. The specific nature of this detail may have

Above **Sestertius** of the Emperor Hadrian, *c.* AD 119. Inscribed AFRICA. Brass. British Museum, London. BMC 1707.

Opposite **Boadicea**, 1856-1902. Thomas Thornycroft. Bronze. Victoria Embankment, London. © Kat Kallou / Alamy Stock Photo.

Below **As** of the Emperor Hadrian, *c.* AD 119. Copper. British Museum, London. 1935,0404.57 as BMC 1175.

symbolic connotations, but has no literary and little archaeological evidence to support it.[6] However, this may be a case in which coins provide the evidence otherwise lacking in other forms of documentation. The spike has become popularly associated with the axles of British chariots, and those of Boudicca in particular, as understood in popular history. It was made famous in the late nineteenth-century bronze figure of *Boadicea* begun in 1856 and completed in 1902 by Thomas Thornycroft, on Victoria Embankment, opposite the Houses of Parliament at Westminster Bridge.[7] The Queen of the rebellious Iceni, supported by her daughters, drives a two-horsed chariot, with wheels embellished with exaggeratedly long scythe-like spikes more Scythian or Persian than British.

The ideas behind the imagery of personification, and, from our point of view that of Britannia, had already found expression in other imperial projects, such as the relief on a giant keystone thought to be from the previous Emperor Trajan's Forum, which was being built when Hadrian came to power in AD 117. This seated figure has been known variously as *Dacia*, *Germania*, *Conquered* or *Weeping Province*, and was used in modern times as a pedestal for a figure of *Roma*.[8] It appears as an appropriately Classical prop in portraits by Pompeo Batoni painted for Scottish and English Grand Tourists, such as the eccentric huntsman Peter Beckford and Douglas Hamilton, 8th Duke of Hamilton, in Rome in the mid eighteenth century.[9] Less ostentatiously the composition appears on Wedgwood and Coadestone plaques at the end of the eighteenth century. Further, it was a source of inspiration for lines in Byron's *Childe Harold*:

> *She their Dacian mother, he their sire,*
> *Butchered to make a Roman holiday.*[10]

Numismatists and historians have identified a marked stylistic change in art under Hadrian, an aesthetic renaissance which coincided with his determined policy to restore the values of Greek civilisation to the Roman Empire. Britannia appears at this early stage in Hadrian's reign to be a fusion of the realism of Rome and the elegance of the Greek aesthetic.[11] An iconographic source for the reverse of the coin may be the silver tetradrachm of Lysimachus of Thrace, one of Alexander the Great's generals. Surely one of the most beautiful of Greek coins, finely modelled it has on its obverse the profile head of Alexander,[12] while on the reverse is the seated figure of Athena, the virgin goddess of arts, crafts, war and ships.

The personification of the city-state as a woman had been established with the identification and adoption of Pallas Athena as the matronal deity of Athens and the Athenian people. Later, as Minerva the goddess of Wisdom, she became part of the iconography of the Roman Republic, transformed into the matronal deity of the city as *Roma*. Here on the reverse of the coin of Lysimachus, Athena is presented in a finely observed warlike fashion: helmeted, bare-breasted, usually seated on a throne or pile of weapons, and holding out the winged figure of Victory, the Nike. The shield, on which she leans her left arm, is decorated with a lion-maned mask; behind her, ready to her right hand, is a downturned lance.[13] She is a prototype for Britannia in every detail. This Alexandrine source probably has an earlier antecedent on coins in the seated figures of Zeus who, according to legend and propaganda, was the progenitor of Alexander himself. These in turn probably have yet earlier eastern seated hieratic figures as their source, while ultimately they are preceded by three-dimensional seated deities or votive figures in sculptural form.

After a number of recorded rebellions, and the mysterious fate of the Hispanic IXth Legion at about that time, the underlying symbolism of Britannia as a Roman province must be one of defence and control.[14] Almost immediately after her first appearance, Hadrian issued coins known today as the 'provincial series', often with the inscription beginning *Restitutori* ('to the restorer of'), and followed by the name of the province, in which were emblematically described the visitations the Emperor planned to make throughout the Empire.[15] Soon he came to Britain, and construction of his eponymous wall began in AD 122. Hadrian celebrated the armies, including that of Britain, with another series of coins. The legend on this type of *sestertius* reads: EXERC.BRITAN. or EXERC.BRITANNICUS, referring directly to Hadrian's British army.[16] Nevertheless, Rome had decided not to undertake the subjugation of North Britain or Caledonia,[17] and Hadrian's Wall, stretching 80 miles from Wallsend in North Tyneside in the east to the Solway Firth in the west, 'qui barbaros Romanosque divideret' ('which divided the Romans and the barbarians'), was as pointedly defensive as those of China or Berlin, although trade was conducted through it. It has been argued by Jocelyn Toynbee and others that Britannia as she appears on this type is not a *capta* type, a figure of subjection, and that far from mourning her lost independence she looks out across the wall, alert and ready to defend the boundaries of the Empire.[18]

This interpretation follows a line of thinking that sees the Hadrianic series of coins as propaganda on the part of the Emperor, whose family was from another Roman province, Spain, to draw the Empire together and bind the margins to the centre.[19] This was not simply *realpolitik*, a pragmatic solution to an ever-expanding frontier, but in design terms it expressed Hadrian's philhellenism and the revival during the Antonine dynasty of Greek ideals in art and culture.[20] An example of this artistic reversion, and another possible source for the iconography of the Britannia coins of Hadrian and Antoninus Pius, may be the figure of a veiled, cross-legged woman, pensively seated on a rubble stone wall or bench, known as *Penelope*, copied in Rome in the first century, after a now lost late fifth century BC Greek figure.[21] This was an image that would become symbolic of the faithful grieving widow on funeral monuments by British Neo-Classical sculptors such as John Flaxman, Sir Francis Chantrey and E. H. Baily at the beginning of the nineteenth century.[22]

Above Sestertius of Hadrian, c. AD 134-5. Brass (enlarged). British Museum, London. BMC 1723.

Opposite Tetradrachm of Lysimachus, King of Thrace. Silver (enlarged). British Museum, London. 1919,0820.1.

Below Penelope, a copy made in Rome in the first century AD. Marble. Sala delle Muse, Vatican Museum, Rome. Alinari / Bridgeman Images.

Roman aesthetics and art tended to realism, whereas the Greek tradition was one of idealism. On the coinage one can detect a fusion of these opposing ideas as the now anonymous artists in Rome worked on the design of a new type of personification: for example, in the earliest type Britannia's hair is not neatly caught up with a fillet and knot or bun, but flows back in loose waves, which suggests an element of realism symbolising a little known and uncivilised province. A similar reappraisal of Greek aesthetics would occur when from the middle of the eighteenth century the Classical archaeologist and early art historian Johann Joachim Winckelmann (1717-68) and other commentators began to distinguish between the Greek and Roman styles,[23] and sculptors and architects such as Canova and Flaxman, C. R. Cockerell and Decimus Burton set out to express what they saw in the Greek style as superior to the Roman.

Under Hadrian's successor Antoninus Pius, whose turf wall between the Forth and the Clyde marked a cautious expansion of territory, a *sestertius* of AD 143 and an *as* of AD 154-5, the latter struck in large numbers, circulated mainly in Britain. The influence of the earliest Hadrianic type is clear.[24] The Antonine types follow that of the Hadrianic in portraying Britannia not as subdued and sorry for herself, but as an active and energetic member of the Empire at a distant outpost of civilisation. On a further type Britannia sits on a globe which floats on what appear to be rippling waves – the sea? If so, this is as direct a reference to her island state as any, one which was to become in modern times a defining feature of Britannia on the coinage.[25] The issue of AD 143 probably reflects events on the ground, at the time when the governor of Britain, Lollius Urbicus, pushed the frontier further north and established the Antonine wall. This successful offensive against the Britons led to Antoninus Pius being acclaimed as Emperor for a second time, and these three variants of a 'vigilant' Britannia, idealised in the Greek tradition, were produced.[26] In marked contrast, the second issue of Britannia types under Antoninus Pius in AD 154-5 perhaps coincides with the crushing of a serious uprising by the Brigantes, and the decision to send legionaries to Britain from Germany under Julius Verus. Now, indeed, we have a *Britannia capta*: disarmed, her spiked shield and *vexillum* or standard is away to the left of the coin, and she the picture of dejection.

In response to a further period of unrest and a punitive expedition in AD 185, a handsome bronze medallion of the Emperor Commodus was struck.[27] Here, however, the image is a repeat of the Antonine Britannia of AD 143, vigilant, one foot raised as though prepared to get up, arms at the ready. The name of the province is misspelt BRITTANIA. The rare *sestertii* of Commodus struck in AD 184-5 depict a standing figure holding a helmet and what is probably a sword, identified by the similarly misspelt abbreviation BRITT.[28] Ironically, when Clodius Albinus, the Governor of Britain, having the legions of Britain and Hispania behind him laid claim to the *imperium* on the assassination of Commodus, it was a seated helmeted *Roma* holding the *pallium* or mantle and sceptre that appeared on the reverse of *denarii*. These were struck at Rome, presumably as part of the deal brokered with Septimius Severus which gave Clodius Albinus dominion over his power base in the northern and western Empire. Nevertheless, not content with that, he marched on Rome, but facing annihilating defeat at Lugdunum, modern Lyons, he committed suicide.[29] The coins of Septimius Severus, Caracalla and Geta that commemorate their later British campaigns of AD

208-11 usually do so with Victory figures on their reverses, even when the legend specifically refers to Britain. On some coins of Septimius Severus a figure which can probably be identified as a standing Britannia appears, occasionally in a hooded cloak or *birrus*. Antiquarians associated this with the Druids, but in the third century it was no doubt worn by anyone who could afford it in a northern climate. Septimius Severus campaigned in Scotland as far north as the Moray Firth, and carried out restoration work on Hadrian's Wall. He died at York in the winter of AD 211.

A very different Britannia appears at the end of the third century on the extraordinary coinage of the rogue emperor, the Romano-Belgian usurper Marcus Aurelius Mausaeus Carausius, and on that of his assassin and successor Allectus.[30] These coins provide vivid visual evidence for much otherwise uncharted history. Some silver coins, today known as *denarii*, carry very specific inscriptions or legends such as *Restitutor Britanniae* ('restorer of Britain') and *Genius Britanniae* ('Spirit of Britain'). Some of these exceptional coins issued by Carausius carry a quotation from Virgil's *Aeneid*, 'Expectate veni' ('come long-awaited one'). Others include the legends RSR and INPCDA in the *exergue*, abbreviations of the sixth and seventh lines of Virgil's *Fourth Eclogue*: 'Redeunt Saturnia Regna, Iam Nova Progenies Caelo Demittitur Alto' ('the Golden Ages return, now a new generation is sent from Heaven above'). As famous in the Roman world as Shakespeare today, quoting Virgil at the extremities of the Empire over 300 years after his death was a knowing gesture, and evidence of the success of Agricola's policy of encouraging:

> a people...prone to fight, to grow pleasurably inured to peace and ease...He trained the sons of the chiefs in the liberal arts...The result was that in place of distaste for the Latin language came a passion to command it.[31]

This would become a hallmark of British understanding of civilisation and culture in modern times that directly affected education in this country, and the development of the design of the coinage.

The obverse of the coins of Carausius portrays the successful leader wearing the victor's laurel wreath or the Emperor's radiate crown. The reverse type depicts the self-styled Emperor shaking the hand of a figure, arguably a standing Britannia, but which might well be a *Pax* or possibly a *Providentia* (Peace or Providence). The standing female figure holds a sceptre. This standing type, if Britannia it is, is not however one that is taken up again until very much later in the evolution of the use of the Britannia image on British coinage, as in the pattern *Peace Crown* of George V in the 1920s. By then the sources are probably less specifically Romano-British ones, and there is little or no evidence that the antiquarians of the seventeenth and eighteenth centuries, whose knowledge informed the iconography of the coinage, were familiar with this exceptional type.

The value of these coins was small, and excluding the gold *aureus* and the silver *denarius* on which the image of Britannia seems never to have appeared, the smaller denominations, the *sestertius* and its fractions, the *dupondius* and the *as*, were usually made from brass alloys and copper respectively. It is noteworthy that the first Britannia appeared on the smallest denomination of coin, although gradually the generic image was used on denominations of increasing value. The inference here is that these coins were the currency of everyday usage, the official tokens of domestic exchange. This presents a parallel in the existence of Britannia on modern British coins in the past 300 years: for though in reality coins of this type were exceptionally rare, in theory the image of Britannia occurred on the small change available to everyone, and in everyday use.

Above Denarius of Carausius, inscribed EXPECTATE VENI. Silver (enlarged). British Museum, London. 1900,1105.10.

Below Medallion of Carausius. *c.* AD 287. Copper alloy (enlarged). British Museum, London. 1972,0717.1.

BRITANNIA

OCEA:
NUS DEVCALI

OCEANUS

Eludes

Cernalij
Carnon ace
CALEDO Canta
NII

GERMANI:

DONIVS

Novartes Olladim
Darnij
Voluntij Bri:
HIBER gan:
Monana tes
Eblana CVS
OCEANUS Eboracum

NIA Mona Deua Cori
HI: Ordo tani
BER: ui
ces Cernauij Iceni
Silures
NICUS Cattechla Trinobantes Tamlis
Sabrina um
Belga Londinum
Durotri Cantium
Danmoni

Vectis

OCEANUS BRI:
TANNICUS

Chapter 3
'Minerva Britanna'

Contrary to popular understanding, the reuse of the image of a seated female warrior is first encountered in the modern world not on British coinage, but on French.[1] In 1555 the personification of the Roman province of Gallia appears on the reverse of a *Henri d'or* and its *demi*,[2] its source the reverse of coins of the Emperor Trajan.[3] In this sophisticated quotation from the antique we may perhaps see the influence of Henri II's wife, the powerful figure of Catherine de Medici, who brought to the French Court from Florence the secular humanism of the late Renaissance with its pervading influence of the classical world. Another rival influence may have been that of the King's *maitresse en titre*, Diane de Poitiers, a significant and educated patron of the arts.

On his accession in 1547, Henri II turned to modernising the French Mint by introducing new designs and new machinery from Germany and Italy. The dies for these gold coins may have been designed by the goldsmith and medallic engraver of Italian origin, Étienne Delaune.[4] A number of his designs depict a woman with familiar attributes of shield, pennant lance, and floriated stem, one inscribed MINERVA GALLIARUM. None are so closely related to the design as it appears on the reverse of the *Henri d'or*, but perhaps, having been selected, the chosen design disappeared into the workshops as a working drawing. The gold patterns were engraved under the direction of Marc Béchot, who had trained under Italian gem engravers, and were struck at the Moulin des Étuves in Paris.[5] These coins are of a very fine quality that retain the precision and, one might say, the modernity of their appearance. It seems these did pass into circulation,[6] but being of high value were probably hoarded or collected from the outset, and cannot be said with any certainty to have had an influence on coin design. Ironically, for political and social reasons, the French were unable to take advantage of the processes they had developed, and it was the British, more than a century later, who, under the émigré French master-engineer and moneyer Pierre Blondeau, developed the technology.

The notion of Britannia as both a place extant in antiquity, and as a personification, had been developed at the end of the sixteenth and beginning of the seventeenth centuries, as part of the polemic leading up to and continued after the unification of Britain under James VI and I in 1603. It was John Dee, the mathematician, geographer, and scholar, adviser to both Elizabeth I and to the maritime adventurers of her reign, who first resurrected Britannia 'as the personification of an empire based on maritime endeavour'.[7] The frontispiece to Dee's *General and Rare Memorials Pertayning to the Perfect Arte of Navigation*, published in 1577, depicted 'RES-Publ. Brytanica, on her knees' whose 'Pyth, or Intent' was an appeal to Queen Elizabeth I to establish a navy or fully-equipped expeditionary force. This provided the embryonic justification for an imperialist expansion into North America, for as Dee put it, it would 'make us, also, Partakers of Publik Commodities Innumerable, and (as yet) Incredible'.[8] Little did he know how incredible.

Above Designs for jetons of Charles IX: seated Minerva figure with Medusa shield, inscribed VIRTUTI REGIS GAL; seated woman in armour with lance, inscribed VIRTUTI FORTUNA CEDIT. Étienne Delaune. Pencil and wash on paper (enlarged). Ashmolean Museum, Oxford. WA.1863.133.131, WA.1863.133.129.

Opposite Frontispiece to William Camden, *Britannia*, 6th edition, 1607. William Hole. Engraving. The Queen's College, Oxford. 53.G.20.

In *Britannia,* first published in 1586, William Camden, the father of antiquarianism and archaeology in Britain, set out to describe in Latin the topography and history of the British Isles, with a sub-text to resurrect the name of Britain and establish her claims to a Classical past.[8] The sixth edition in 1607, still in Latin, referred to Roman coins in *Notae ad Romanorum Numismata*.[9] The reverse of the Antonine coins are described thus by Camden: 'in aversis partibus alter Britanniam rupibus insidentem cum signo militari, hasta, & scuto, alter eandem globo insidentem habet'.[10] This edition carried a frontispiece engraved by William Hole, who in 1618 would become Engraver to the Mint. Here Hole presents Britannia for the first time, in a cartouche, clearly based on the reverse of coins of Antoninus Pius in the group of engravings entitled *Nummi Antiqui Romanorum*, also by him, that accompanied the edition.

The first edition in English in 1610 was translated by Philemon Holland and published in 1610 as *Britain, or a Chorographicall description of the most flourishing Kingdomes, England, Scotland, and Ireland, and the Ilands adioyning, out of the depth of Antiquitie*.[11] It was much praised at the time for popularising something hitherto unreadable by non-Classicists.[12] The figure on the frontispiece is decidedly androgynous, and could as well be a young male figure, Britannia in chrysalis, not yet evolved into her matronal figure. This may indeed be because in the reign of Elizabeth I, the Virgin Queen, a separate identity for Britannia might be confusing, possibly even traitorous, and in many ways unnecessary. As recent historians have made clear, there is no doubt that Elizabeth, married (as she would have her subjects believe) to her country, could be identified as Britannia herself.[13]

Britannia had an alter ego in Minerva, the Roman Goddess of Wisdom, and in terms of presentation and attributes these two are often indistinguishable, save that Minerva is more often shown standing. There are ten allegorical figures or virtues on the wall monument to Sir Thomas Bodley in Merton College Chapel, Oxford, designed by the Flemish-trained sculptor Nicholas Stone. The small standing figure in the broken pediment is Minerva, in one of her manifestations as Goddess of Wisdom, as befits the founder of a great university library. Her lance and shield, however, are also attributes of Britannia.[14] This ambiguity recurs across the next two centuries at the University of Oxford. The title page of the learned Dr Plot's *The Natural History of Staffordshire* published in 1686 announces Plot as 'Professor of Chymistry' in the University and Keeper of the Ashmolean Museum, and Minerva as 'the Genius of Antique Learning'.[15] Each year the University almanack or calendar had a distinguished engraving at its head. In celebration of the presentation to the University of the Arundel Marbles by the Countess of Pomfret two years earlier, the dual personality appears for the year 1757.[16]

Henry Peacham is best known for his essentially English imitation of Castiglione's *The Courtier*,[17] *The Compleat Gentleman* (1622),[18] a handbook for the socially and culturally aspirant. His book of emblems *Minerva Britanna or a Garden of Heroical Devises* addressed to Henry, Prince of Wales in 1612, made several references to the Roman source for the image of Britannia. The dedicatory verses made play with the duality of Pallas (Athena)/Minerva and Britannia.[19] The emblem of Britannia bestriding sea and land, one foot on a ship and one on shore is altogether more assertive than that described in the first verse of the *impresa*:

> Thus Britaine's drawn in old Antiquities,
> What time the Romanes overran her land:
> Who first devis'd her, sitting in this plight,
> As then their captive, and abandon'd quite.
>
> But what can long continue at a stay,
> To all things being, Fates a change decree:
> Thrice-famous Ile, whome erst thou didst obey,
> Usurping Roome, standes now in aw of thee[20]

Here Peacham refers specifically to a design, devised and drawn, and his source appears to be unequivocally a 'capta' type coin: 'sitting in this plight', a Roman captive, 'abandon'd quite'. This would suggest that he and others were looking at the Antonine type of AD 155. The subtext is the recurrent theme of national antipathy to Catholic and Papal Rome, while, nevertheless, adopting Roman precedents from the antique. James VI and I, and his sons Henry and Charles, in their determination to unite Scotland and England, were happy to adopt ideas that took their dynastic claims beyond a Christianity that was Augustine and therefore Roman, to a mythic Classical foundation by the Trojan Brutus, to Joseph of Arimathea and the Arthurian legends; the very word Britannia, it was claimed, was

Above **The Natural History of Staffordshire**, 1686. Robert Plot. Bodleian Library, Oxford. Lister D 50.

Hebrew for the Land of God's Covenant.[21] In the fine frontispiece to Michael Drayton's 15,000 line topographical poem *Poly-Olbion*, which with the illustrative maps was also engraved by William Hole, Brutus and Julius Caesar stare at each other above the figure of Great Britaine. This proto-Britannia, her hair elegantly unkempt, sits on a rock and holds a sceptre and a cornucopia of carefully arranged fruit and ears of corn. She is draped in a map, which closely resembles one of a series of tapestry maps, known as Sheldon tapestries after their maker Ralph Sheldon,[22] while behind stretches the sea and a number of bobbing boats.

Drayton had collaborated with the antiquarian John Selden on his epic descriptions, and it was Selden's *Mare Clausum* (1618, published 1635), which provided the intellectual argument for claims over the sea. This was written as a riposte to *Mare Liberum* (1609) in which Hugo Grotius made the case for the Dutch claim to the North Sea and beyond. Selden's defence of Britain's naval supremacy cited the coinage of Antoninus Pius as an antique precedent, based on his mistaken, but convenient reading of what were rocks as waves on the engraved illustrations of coins in Camden. However, it is possible that William Hole, Camden's engraver, and Selden were both looking at the rarer Antonine *sestertius* of AD 143. Whether the source was primary or secondary, this neat interpretation would cast a long shadow, and waves have continued to play an irregular, but persistent part in the design of the coinage.

In the cultural renaissance that characterised the reigns of the first two Stuart Kings it was the Flemings, Peter Paul Rubens and Anthony Van Dyck, the Frenchman Hubert Le Seuer,[23] and the Englishman with Welsh antecedents Inigo Jones, all of whom were well versed in the antique, who established an English Court style. In Rubens' great painted ceiling in Jones' Banqueting House in Whitehall, the apotheosis of the reign of James VI and I which glorifies the King's wisdom and the benefits of the reign, a vigorously active Minerva appears in every triptych sequence, sometimes twice. Minerva might be taken for a proto-Britannia, joining the crown over the head of an infant boy between England and Scotland, usually understood to be the male progenitor of the new dynasty, the future Charles I.[24] Rubens and Van Dyck, the latter particularly in his equestrian imagery of Charles I, which took its inspiration from the bronze figure of Marcus Aurelius on the Capitoline Hill in Rome, presented monarchy as monarchy might hope to be presented. A more light-hearted, but in its way equally serious, manifestation of the idea of Britannia emerged in one of the innovations of the artistically dynamic Stuart Court, first under the aegis of James VI and I's wife Anne of Denmark and later under that of her son, Charles I.[25] This was the masque, with its poetry, music and dance. The leading exponents of this dramatic art form were Ben Jonson and Inigo Jones. The latter had travelled in Italy in his youth and later, from 1612 to 1614, with Thomas Howard, Earl of Arundel, known as the 'Collector Earl', in search of the remains of the Classical world.[26]

One of the final masques before the start of the Civil War was the annual Twelfth Night masque of 1638. Designed by Jones and sung by William Davenant, it was entitled *Britannia Triumphans*.[27] A confusion between Minerva and Britannia is detectable in the standing figure in armour in Jones' costume design, in which the Goddess of Wisdom is also combative. Davenant was made Poet Laureate on the death of Ben Jonson in 1638, but the sense of outrage that such dramatic revelries and their huge cost induced in Puritans probably contributed to his being later sentenced

to death and imprisoned in the Tower of London. John Milton's *Comus* (c.1638) expressed this collective disgust with Court licentiousness in allegorical form. However Milton, poet of the Commonwealth and adviser to Oliver Cromwell, is said to have intervened on Davenant's behalf, and the latter was to return to Court at the Restoration in 1660. The ideas behind the political, social and artistic polemic of the late sixteenth and early seventeenth centuries could be said to have entered the bloodstream of the ruling classes. With the establishment of a constitutional monarchy under Charles II and an authoritative coinage, Britannia was about to enter the bloodstream of the nation as a whole.

Charles II's exile on the Continent had acquainted him with technical developments, such as the milling process, which gave strips of metal a necessary all-over evenness, and the screw presses which replaced the skilled manual hammer. The verb 'to strike' had given a name to the process that survives, although the technology moved on. Living at The Hague in Holland, Charles and members of his Court-in-exile will have been familiar with exceptionally high quality medals and coins. One of these, a silver medal by an unknown Dutch artist of 1655, is decidedly ambivalent in its message, but certainly satirical. On the obverse Oliver Cromwell is presented crowned with laurel. On the reverse, however, Britannia gestures to the bare rump of a kneeling figure identified as Cromwell, his head in her lap, while two overdressed fellows pantomime an 'Allow me/After you, Claude' moment.[28] This is the earliest appearance of Britannia on a medal in modern

times. Another, also struck in 1655, is for Amsterdam, on which ships, some firing a salute, and church spires form a backdrop to the personification of Amsterdam sitting in a rope stockade. She, crowned, holds an olive branch and shield initialled SPQA ('the Senate and People of Amsterdam'), itself adapted from the motto of the Roman Republic SPQR: *Senatus Populusque Romanus*, while two kittenish lions clutch at heraldic shields. There was food for thought here, as the Dutch Republic would become rivals with Britain in the reassertion of national ambitions. It is therefore no surprise to find in 1662 Charles recalling Pierre Blondeau who had brought his 'secret' edging machines to London from Paris during the Commonwealth, but had achieved limited success under Oliver Cromwell. Blondeau's grained and lettered edges helped prevent clipping, cutting the irregularities around the coin edges that amounted to stealing of little pieces of gold and silver from the coinage, and thus devaluing it. Medallic engravers of the calibre of John, Joseph and Philip Roettiers were invited from Antwerp when in 1660 the reform of the coinage was begun.

Chapter 4

In competition with the ancient masters

After a period of acute social and religious unrest in mid seventeenth-century Britain, the imperial coinage of Hadrian and Antoninus Pius became the iconographic source for the new coinage which appeared from 1662 under the newly-established constitutional monarchy of Charles II. This systematic development took advantage of the French failure to adopt new technology, and was part of the ultimately successful policy of creating a national identity in the aftermath of the Restoration, when the calling-in of all Commonwealth coinage had caused an acute shortage of money.

The need for 'small moneys to be currant in low and ordinary payments amongst the poorer sort' was met in 1672 by the King's Proclamation 'for making currant His Majestie's Farthings and Half-pence of Copper, and forbidding all others to be used'.[1] It was profiteering by the counterfeiters and makers of tokens that initiated this response for, as the Proclamation continued:

> our subjects have been greatly defrauded, and our Royal authority and the Laws of our kingdom violated. And whereas We, for the prevention of the like abuses for the time to come, did not only direct a severe prosecution of the offenders, but did likewise command the officers of our Mint to cause many thousands of pounds of good sterling silver to be coined into single pence and twopences, so that there might be good money currant among the poorest of our subjects, and fitted for their small traffic and commerce; ... since which time we have found by experience, that the mischief hath still encreased, partly by having our small silver money bought in and hoarded up, ... we ... have thought fit, by advice of our Privy Council, to cause certain farthings and halfpence of copper to be stamped at our Mint, according to such form and with such impression as we have directed.[2]

From 1674 farthings and halfpennies were officially issued from the Farthing Office on Fenchurch Street.[3]

The response to this Proclamation has been described as nothing less than revolutionary, both in terms of production and administration.[4] The appearance of Britannia on the reverse of some of the coins of Charles II from 1672 coincided with two related factors: technical advances in manufacture, and the employment of new designers. There were three significant developments in the mechanisation of production: the introduction, in preparation for making the blanks, of milling, involving horse-powered rolling-mills to process ingots into strips; and Pierre Blondeau's screw-press and 'secret' edge-marking machine, which had been rejected by the French. As the numismatist Charles Peck so succinctly put it,

Above **Halfpenny of Charles II, 1672. John Roettiers. Copper.** RMM718.

Opposite **Farthing of Charles II, pattern, 1665, inscribed** QUATUOR MARIA VINDICO. **John Roettiers. Copper (enlarged).** RMM718.

Blondeau was to provide 'all the necessary machinery for rolling, cutting, and rounding the blanks, and for lettering or graining their edges'.[5] These developments now undoubtedly gave an advantage to the Crown monopoly at the moment of consolidation of political change. Both gave the coins a solid, even uniform appearance that must have contributed to the confidence in a unitary monetary system. By gearing up production they helped reduce if not eliminate the periodic shortages of coins that encouraged the use of tokens; these were a sign of retrogressive practices detrimental to a sound national fiscal policy. The need for them as markers of exchange was thus undermined.

Historians of the development of the currency in Britain in the immediate aftermath of 1660 have considerable and pertinent contemporary sources. Probably the most important of these was the diarist, natural philosopher, and antiquarian John Evelyn. His life spanned one of the most radical centuries in terms of the development of human understanding and the place of humankind in the universe. Two portraits, one from early in his life and one from later on, graphically describe this quantum change. In the first Evelyn poses in thoughtful Miltonic melancholy,[6] fashionable in northern European Humanism, calling to mind Dürer's engraving *Melancholia* (1514), one of the most potent images of this form of Neo-Platonism. The early portrait is by Robert Walker, a follower, one might say imitator, of Van Dyck. It is so uncharacteristic of Walker's work that one might conclude it was a highly personal commission: this is how Evelyn, at the age of 28, wanted to be presented, thoughtful, worldly wise, and educated. In the second portrait, 40 years later, Evelyn lightly grasps a book, looking out at us with energetic but calm confidence; from Reformation to Enlightenment, Mannerism to Baroque in one lifetime. As a young man Evelyn had seen Charles I's chief adviser Thomas Wentworth, 1st Earl of Strafford, executed on Tower Hill, in the early stages of what became the Civil War. As a Royalist he failed to take up arms and went into self-imposed exile on the Continent. In Venice in 1645 he met the exiled Earl of Arundel, who much earlier had travelled to Italy with Inigo Jones. Evelyn was advised by the Earl, now old and weary, in 'Remembrances' of what to see in Rome and elsewhere.[7] Evelyn had a cabinet made incorporating the *pietre dure* panels he had acquired in Florence in 1644, to house his collection of coins and medals and his diaries. A comparatively simple example of these most exclusive and grand pieces of furniture – the birds, flowering stems of orange, jasmine, and periwinkle, primroses with botanically incorrect leaves in coloured stones, and animals after Ovid on the gilt bronze plaquettes by Francesco Fanelli – the cabinet befitted its owner: a renaissance man or man of the new empiricism, gardener, horticulturist, author, and founding member of the Royal Society.[8] This learned organisation, to give it its full title the Royal Society of London for Improving Natural Knowledge, perhaps more than any other embodied a new era of constitutional monarchy and scientific progress.

Evelyn made his second tour to Italy in the years 1664-5 and, as his diaries record, made it his business to acquaint himself with the remains of antiquity and to buy 'Medailes & other curiosities, Antiquities &c'.[9] He was well acquainted with other collectors, and with their collections of antique coins;[10] in Rome he had visited Cassiano dal Pozzo's Museo Carteggio or Paper Museum.[11] He was familiar with publications on the subject, William Burton's *A Commentary on Antoninus his Itinerary* (1658), among them. In *Numismata: A Discourse of Medals Antient and Modern*, Evelyn refers to the recent presentation by the Duke of Norfolk to the Royal Society of the collection in 'four noble volumes of *Duke Alberts of Bavaria*'.[12] He himself prospected for coins on his return to England, in a seventeenth-century equivalent of metal detecting, by walking the North Downs between his houses at Deptford and at Wootton in Surrey. On one occasion he described an Arcadian encounter with some shepherds who were probably the source of his 'finds',[13] and on at least two occasions he looked at coins in Bodley's Library in the University of Oxford in 1654 and again in 1664.[14] When he came to write *Numismata*, published in 1697, Evelyn demonstrated his intimate knowledge of antique coinage, and his understanding of its symbolism as a precedent.

Evelyn's diaries suggest a close involvement with the day-to-day activity associated with the reform of the coinage. In January 1662, he was called into the King's Closet 'when Mr. Cooper ... was crayoning of his face & head, to make the stamps by, for the new *Mill'd* mony, now contriving, I had the honour to hold the candle whilst it was doing'. While Samuel Cooper, the miniaturist who earlier had been instructed by Oliver Cromwell to record what he saw, 'warts and all', was drawing the King's portrait, Evelyn and the King talked 'of Painting and Graving &c'.[15] As Cooper was not an engraver, and in mentioning 'the stamps' Evelyn was almost certainly referring to the dies that had to be engraved, it is likely that he and Charles II were discussing the engraver's art as it specifically related to coinage, the business in hand being a portrait of the King for the obverse of the new coinage. On 6 September 1662 Evelyn dined with Sir Edward Walker, Garter King at Arms, and Henry Slingsby, Master of the Mint;[16] then almost a year later with Sir Philip Warwick, Secretary to the Lord Treasurer. Warwick showed him the accounts and 'other private matters relating to the Revenue', before Evelyn went on 'to the Commissioners of the *Mint*, particularly about Coynage',[17] and then home. He records going to the Tower of London again on 9 March 1664, 'to sit in Commission about regulating the Mint, & how it was the fine Milled Coyne both of White-mony & Ginnies was established'.[18] Further meetings of 'our *Mint Commiss*', which sat at the Tower of London, are recorded on 24 April and 10 July 1666.[19]

From these diary entries Evelyn was clearly on familiar terms with Henry Slingsby, the Master of the Mint and a fellow founding member of the Royal Society. It was to him that Evelyn suggested the epigrammatic, anti-counterfeiting inscription *Decus et Tutamen* ('an ornament and a safeguard') for the edge of the five guineas, crown and half-crown in gold and silver.[20] Slingsby descended from a Yorkshire family whose members had, as Courtiers, been part of the cultural renaissance at the end of Elizabeth I's reign, and at the Court of James VI and I at the beginning of the century.[21] It was Slingsby who had encouraged Blondeau when in the 1650s an earlier attempt at mechanisation had met with opposition of the moneyers at the Mint.[22] The fine silver coins bearing Oliver Cromwell's portrait were struck using Blondeau's methods. Now Slingsby initiated Blondeau's return and appointment as engineer to the Mint, with the express intention of improving the production of the coin. As Samuel Pepys recorded it '[Slingsby] says Blondeau will shortly come over, and then we shall have it better, and the best in the world'.[23]

Above **John Evelyn**, 1688. Studio of Godfrey Kneller. Oil on canvas.
© Sotheby's / akg-images.

Evelyn had been commissioned by Charles II to write an account of Anglo-Dutch relations, published in 1674 as *Navigation and Commerce*. In *Numismata* Evelyn expressed a generally-held view that Charles II was:

the most knowing in Naval Affairs, and vigilant to Improve and Maintain the Safety and Glory of these Kingdoms in its highest and chiefest Concern, which is certainly its Strength at Sea.[24]

The low denomination base metal coinage of 1672 was initiated by the Privy Council as an adjunct of the state, and became 'a national currency', after the Act for Encouraging Coinage in 1666. With this Act the Crown became responsible for the costs of making and administering the coinage, these costs to be defrayed by imposts on certain imported goods.[25] Copper coins were now legal tender, being part of the monetary reform which included the suppression of tradesmen's tokens and their replacement by copper halfpennies and farthings.[26] This saw the introduction for the first time of an official copper halfpenny or 'ha'penny' as it became known,[27] whose eventual ubiquity would lend itself to the traditional pub board-game, Shove Ha'penny. It survived decimalisation in 1971, only to be withdrawn in the inflationary 1980s. There were further issues of copper coins in 1673, 1675 and 1679.

The replacement by Charles II in 1661 of Thomas Simon, the engraver at the Mint during the Republic, by the brothers John, Joseph and Philip Roettiers, goldsmith engravers from Antwerp, did not just reflect a change in political climate. Antwerp had been a source for innovation and artistic invention in London since the late sixteenth century, when Flemish masons, settling in Southwark, had created a market and a style that dominated the proliferation of post-Reformation funerary monuments and chimney-pieces of the period.[28] Much of the inspiration for a Court style came from Antwerp

Above *Restoration of the Monarchy*, medal, 1660. John Roettiers. Silver (enlarged). © Christopher Eimer.

with Rubens and his pupil Van Dyck, both of whom were knighted for services to the monarchy. Antwerp was one of the most important centres for the northern Renaissance, and for intellectual enterprise which found its inspiration in Classical antiquity without the taint of Catholic Rome. Humanist ideas were disseminated through books published at the Plantin Press by Christopher Plantin and his extended family of descendants.[29] The city was also the financial hub of trade in northern Europe, and a market for coins, antiquities and paintings. The Roettiers were a dynasty of distinguished die-engravers and medallists, familiar with Continental advances in minting money, and well acquainted with a tradition of Court taste and the significance of the antique. Evelyn described John Roettiers, after a visit to the Tower on 20 July 1678, as:

> that incomparable Graver belonging to the Mint, who emulates even the Antients in both mettal & stone, he was now moulding of an Horse for the Kings statue to be cast in silver of a Yard high.[30]

The political economist William Petty, writing a decade later, attested to the Roettiers' brilliance, noting as he did 'on Account of Beauty our Britannia halfpence were almost all hoarded as medals till they grew common'.[31]

Britannia first appeared on the reverse of a medal to celebrate the Restoration of the monarchy on 29 May 1660 over the inscription FELICITAS.BRITANNIAE, described by Evelyn as 'sitting under a Cliff by the Sea shore, with a Spear in one hand, and the *Union-Shield* in the other'.[32] The design for the reverse of the copper farthings and halfpennies of 1672, may have been connected to an earlier proof or pattern for a copper farthing in 1665. In that year Charles II's brother, James, Duke of York, as Lord High Admiral, defeated the Dutch at sea in the first of three Anglo-Dutch wars. The pattern farthing depicted Britannia for the very first time,

with her name boldly in the exergue, and the ambitious legend *Quatuor Maria Vindico*, 'I claim the four seas'. It was the inscription, considered presumptuous on a base metal coin which was satirised by Lord Lucas in the House of Lords in 1670, in a speech on the scarcity of money. This may have delayed the adoption of the design on the reverse of small denomination currency.[33] It is also possible that it was too overt a claim for Charles II's patron, Louis XIV.[34] The design was then used for what has been described variously as 'an experiment', and as a 'never completed' medal, the so-called *Naval Victories Medal* of 1666-7 by John Roettiers,[35] after the Dutch Admiral Michiel Adriaenszoon de Ruyter had led an alarmingly successful raid up the Thames estuary to within sight of Greenwich. This was the occasion when the Admiralty official and diarist Samuel Pepys in a fit of panic buried his own hoard of coins.[36] The 'experiment' may have been a stage in the design process in which the obverse die, which would no doubt have been the profile portrait of Charles II by Roettiers, did not need changing. Britannia herself is presented in a surprisingly relaxed pose *en negligée*, the pair of *putti* who crown her with a laurel wreath being perhaps a reference to Castor and Pollux, the heavenly twins who, according to maritime tradition, appear heralding calm after a storm. The rayed sun breaking through clouds has a similar surface significance, but also has a number of more sophisticated meanings, being an emblematic device derived from the sixteenth-century theories of the philosopher Giordano Bruno which applied the Copernican theory of heliocentricity, the sun at the centre of the planetary system, to an absolutist nature of kingship.[37] The Stuart dynasty subscribed to this theory of kingship, for, as Thomas Reeves put it in *England's Beauty*, 'a King in a commonwealth is like...the sun in the firmament'.[38] It may also be a tactful acknowledgement of the support of Louis XIV, the Sun King, who took the theory of heliocentricity to extreme lengths.[39]

The design re-emerged as the reverse of the *Peace of Breda* medal, struck to mark the negotiations of 31 July 1667 which brought the Second Dutch War to an end. Here Britannia's previously relaxed air has given way to an altogether more alert pose as, wearing a cuirass or breast-plate, she firmly grasps her lance and shield with its Cross of St George and the Saltire, or St Andrew's Cross. She has her back to a sea cliff as she observes in the near distance a ship, the ship of state, and the fleet, 'the wooden walls',[40] and at a distance to the left, the Dutch fleet. The obverse carries Roettiers' portrait of Charles II, and the edge is inscribed: CAROLUS SECUNDUS PACIS ET IMPERII RESTITUTOR AUGUSTUS ('King Charles II, restorer of peace and kingship'). The words are significant: they convey the idea of monarchy as a unifying symbol, a pax against civil war,[41] and an emphasis on the Restoration of the *imperium* of the Stuarts. There is also a possible reference to the Pax Romana under Hadrian and Antoninus Pius, and specifically in the inscription to the Hadrianic coins inscribed *Restitutori Orbis Terrarum* ('to the restorer of the whole world'). Britannia was a deliberate choice, as Charles II reasserted the Stuart Kings' claim to lordship of the seas. In 1672 the Third Dutch war broke out, with subventions from Louis XIV to Charles II, which may indeed have paid for the issue of the new coinage, just as the purchase of Dunkirk by the French in 1662 had made possible the minting of the higher denominations of gold and silver coins for the new reign.[42]

The suggestion that the figure of Britannia herself was modelled on Frances Teresa Stuart, later Duchess of Richmond, has been considered by some, on grounds of scale, to be myth-making.[43] It has, however, recently been accepted as a proposal on the evidence of four contemporaries, the diarists John Evelyn and Samuel Pepys, and the poets Edmund Waller and Andrew Marvell, all of whom considered Frances Stuart to be Britannia's model.[44] Edmund Waller left no one in doubt in his poem *Upon the Gold Medal*,[45] as to who the sitter for Britannia was, while Andrew Marvell,

Above **Frances Stuart**, *c.* 1667. John Roettiers. Lead, nineteenth-century cast of silver medal. National Portrait Gallery, London. NPG 1681.

Below **Peace of Breda**, medal, 1667. John Roettiers. Silver (enlarged). RMM.

satirising another of Waller's poems, *Instructions to a Painter*, referred openly to Frances Stuart:

> The *Court* in Farthing yet itself does please
> And female *Stewart*, there, Rules the four Seas.
> And Fate does still accumulate our woes,
> And *Richmond* here commands, as Ruyter those.[46]

Frances Stuart was a member of the extended Stuart clan, whose family had followed Charles II into exile in 1649. She grew up at the Court-in-exile in The Hague that centred round Charles I's widow, Henrietta Maria, and came to England as a Maid-of-Honour to Charles II's Queen, Catherine of Braganza, in 1662. In a Court obsessed by beauty and with presentations and representations of allegory and symbol, Frances was well-known not just for her beauty, but also for her Amazonian equestrian skills. As one of the 'Windsor Beauties' she was depicted at the age of 17 in Peter Lely's portrait as Diana the Huntress. Ten years later, now sloe-eyed and dark haired in conformity with the Caroline Court's revised ideal of beauty, and no doubt also the influence of the King's dark-eyed, dark-haired mistress, Louise de Kérouaille, Duchess of Portsmouth,[47] she was painted by the French artist Henri Gascar as Minerva or Pallas Athene. This may itself be a self-conscious reference to her role as Britannia.[48] Samuel Pepys alludes to the presence and beauty at Court of Frances Stuart on a number of occasions, and in 1664 Pepys saw her coming away from a portrait sitting at which the King had been present.[49] She had had the distinction of being drawn not once but several times by the greatest British painter-in-small, Samuel Cooper, in 1662 and 1663, when, as we know from John Evelyn, the King was also sitting to Cooper.[50] Cosimo III de Medici would later try to acquire from the artist's widow, through an agent, a miniature of Frances Stuart, which the Grand Duke had remembered from his visit to London in 1669, when he too had sat to Cooper.[51] There is a uniface silver medal of Frances Stuart by John Roettiers, which bears a close resemblance to the profile head of Britannia on the Breda Medal.[52] In 1667, Pepys recorded:

> at my goldsmith's did observe the King's new Medall where in little there is Mrs Stewards face, as well done as ever I saw anything in my whole life I think – and a pretty thing it is that he should choose her face to represent Britannia by.[53]

Techniques of modelling change little, and it is likely that John Roettiers modelled a profile portrait of Frances Stuart in either wax or clay, but most probably in wax on a sheet of slate, as is still done today by medallists. Comparing favourably the Roettiers' designs with those on the reverse of coins of Hadrian and others 'so exquisitely designed', Evelyn continued:

> *Monsieur Roti* (Graver to his late Majesty Charles II) so accurately express'd the countenance of the *Dutchess* of R – in the Head of *Britannia*, in the Reverse of some of our Coin, and especially in a *Medal*, as one may easily, and almost at first sight, know it to be her Grace: And tho in smallest *Copper*...such as may justly stand in competition with the antient Masters.[54]

Above **Honeybees**, illustration to
Fables of La Fontaine, Paris, 1668.
François Chauveau. Engraving.

Opposite Bank of England
running cash notes dated 1697
and 1700. © The Governor and Company
of the Bank of England.

And here we have the answer to the riddle of the question of scale: how could so small a likeness be achieved? If one considers Roman imperial coinage over 300 years, what is most apparent is the immediate impression that one is looking at a portrait gallery in small: the specifics of portrait likeness and characterisation are all there. These are not generic heads in profile, not the *beau-ideal* of Classical beauty, or even an idealisation of an image. For all their individual repetitiveness they are clearly likenesses, and subscribe to the albeit anachronistic Cromwellian dictum: 'warts and all'.

The strength and beauty of the coinage of Henry VII of about 1504, and that of Henry's grandson Edward VI in the mid sixteenth century, are in the likeness of their profile portraits. In 1494 Henry, with the permission of the Emperor Lewis or Ludwig IV Duke of Bavaria, had invited the goldsmith Alexander of Bruchsal to act as Chief Engraver at the Mint in the Tower of London, with the express intention of improving the portrait images of the King. Henry VII's coinage symbolised the consolidation of the country under the new Tudor dynasty at the end of the Wars of the Roses.[55] The fine silver coins of Edward VI present the boy-king as a Renaissance prince.[56] Difficult as it is to capture childish features, these fine coins may well have been among the sources used by eighteenth-century sculptors in historicising busts, which manage to avoid the strong stylistic taint of anachronism.[57] The most sophisticated medallists could and did achieve a likeness however reduced in scale.

The skills and the slow deliberate processes involved in making new dies meant that reverse designs were not quick to change and both James II and William III continued to use the reverse types of their predecessor. James' reign was short and highly unstable, while William was so occupied for most of the reign with extirpating any opposition to the Protestant ascendancy that despite the fiduciary currency theories of the empirical philosopher John Locke,[58] and the Great Recoinage undertaken in the 1690s,[59] little change is observable in the designs. Such, however, was the success of their manner and style in disseminating popular and aesthetic propaganda that while some of the members of the Roettiers' dynasty retired to Antwerp, Joseph Roettiers was invited to Paris by Jean-Baptiste Colbert, Louis XIV's Controller General of Finance, Secretary of State for the Navy and the most powerful man in France. Joseph became Engraver-General of coins in 1682, and as one of the first to contribute to the *Medallic Histories* which record the achievements of the reign of Louis XIV, he was given the title of Premier Graveur de l'Histoire en Médailles.

The success of the establishment of Britannia as the matriarchal embodiment of a nation was confirmed when, in 1694, the newly-founded Bank of England took her as its identifying device or emblem, what today would undoubtedly be called a 'logo'.[60] Britannia appears on the Bank's Common Seal from the outset, the Court of Directors having decided she should be 'sitting or looking on a Bank of money', so that the emblem was at once a rebus or heraldic pun. Britannia has been present on all promissory notes, bills of exchange, and notes issued by the Bank of England since.[61] Even the watermark in the Bank's writing paper was a Britannia. The heaps of coins, in place of the piles of stones of antiquity, come and go, to be not infrequently replaced by bees and bee skips, for as the psalm implies they are as one in terms of value: 'More to be desired ... than gold, yea, than much fine gold: sweeter also than honey and the honeycomb'.[62] Bees have from ancient times been associated with industry and prosperity, abstract

N.º 223

Received of Mr George Martin in New money
the Summe of Two hundred & Six pounds Eleven shill & 10 d
with promise to repay to him or Bearer on demand in y same
Specie with a half Penny a day Interest for each twenty
five Pounds for any time not exceeding One Year London y
2 day of October 1697

£206: 11: 10

For the Govr & Compa
of the Bank of England.

Thomas Madox

N.º ____

Promise to pay to the Bishop of Chichester on Bearer
on Demand the Summe of One hundred & fifty Pound
London the 18 Day of May 1700

For the Govr & Compa of
the Bank of England.

Joseph Ple

£150
100
50

Bo the Manning

ideas that had been encapsulated in Aesop's fables. The late seventeenth century and early eighteenth century saw a burgeoning of the genre of moralising story-telling both in Britain and on the Continent,[63] such as the fables of La Fontaine, illustrated by François Chauveau and published in 1668. The adoption of the bee skip instead of a heap of coins as more elevated in emblematic terms was probably a conscious decision, although there is the possibility that initially at least the one evolved out of the other, the result of poor draughtsmanship or even of poor eyesight. The Bank of England's original and anonymous engraver was clearly not of the stature of those at the Mint, and the domed pile of money is easily to be confused or accepted as a straw beehive.[64]

In the early days the Bank did not have its own premises, and occupied rooms in the Grocers' Hall, outside which swung a wooden sign incorporating Britannia.[65] In the 1730s a new building was planned on Lothbury, with the involvement of Theodore Jacobsen,[66] Master of the Hansa Steelyard, and an amateur architect, who was engaged in building projects associated with the notion of Britannia, such as the East India Company and the Foundling Hospital. The first buildings were completed, however, by George Sampson in 1732-4,[67] with a high relief Britannia in the pediment of the Great or Pay Hall, attributed either to Sir Robert Taylor or Sir Henry Cheere, or both.[68] As Taylor was an apprentice in Cheere's workshop at the time of the commission, the style is predominantly that of the workshop. The commission by the Governors of the Bank of two statues from Cheere was reported in the *Whitehall Evening Post* in November 1733, *Britannia* 'being the distinction or seal of that company', in Portland stone, *William III* in marble.[69] The vigorously proactive image is quite unlike others, and bears a strong resemblance to Minerva, as presented in 1731 and 1733 by William Kent and Michael Rysbrack on the monuments to Sir Isaac Newton and James Ist Earl Stanhope in the nave of Westminster Abbey.

Taylor was responsible for the extension of these original buildings from 1766 to 1788.[70] He became Surveyor of the Bank of England, the Foundling Hospital, the Admiralty, Greenwich Hospital and Lincoln's Inn. Britannia remained on her pediment in the inner courtyard throughout the early nineteenth-century rebuilding programme conducted to the designs of Sir John Soane. Most of Sampson and Taylor's buildings were ruthlessly swept away in the expansion of the Bank from 1921 to 1937 to designs by Sir Herbert Baker.[71] Britannia, however, survived and now resides above the inner entrance in a magnificent if inaccessible ensemble at the Lothbury Gate.[72] In 'The Lady of the Bank', the persona of Britannia had become that of the Bank itself.

Above *Britannia*, 1855. Daniel Maclise. Versions of this Britannia appeared on Bank of England notes issued between 1855 and 1956. © The Governor and Company of the Bank of England.

Opposite *Britannia*, 1739. Sir Robert Taylor or Sir Henry Cheere. Stone. Lothbury Gate, Bank of England. © The Governor and Company of the Bank of England.

Chapter 5
For the use of trade

Introduced as a symbol of Crown authority in 1672 under Charles II, and retained under William III as one of constitutional monarchy, Britannia in the Roettiers' manner remained a stable and consistent emblem on British low-denomination base-metal coinage throughout the eighteenth century. This had become necessary because in the previous century, and indeed the eighteenth, unofficial copper alloy tokens made by private manufacturers were in circulation. Britannia stood out on the reverse as distinctly different from the more usual heraldic devices, which, being complex in their significance, may have eluded general understanding. As an immediately identifiable image Britannia already carried authority and confidence. Stylistically she satisfied post-Baroque Augustan Classicism well into the middle of the eighteenth century and beyond. By the 1730s, Britannia had become firmly embedded in the nation's psyche, for the richer on every promissory note, for the poorer on every copper coin. An easily recognisable symbol in everyone's pocket, Britannia contributed greatly to the establishment of patriotic awareness, and it may be said she was the single, most effective, and immediate means of establishing a newly conjoined national identity.

The Master of the Mint under Queen Anne was none other than that scientist associated with the apple, and known thus to every schoolchild, Sir Isaac Newton. As Master, Newton experimented with the copper medium of the coinage,[1] and considered the issue of new designs for the halfpennies and farthings by the master engraver, John Croker. Croker came from Dresden, arriving via the Low Countries in 1691, and in 1697 succeeded James Roettiers as assistant to Henry Harris the Chief Engraver at the Royal Mint. On Harris' death in 1704, Croker successfully petitioned for the post, and remained at the Mint until his own death in 1741. His time there was marked by the distinction of the many medals made to record events of national importance, such as the *Union of England and Scotland* of 1707, and the *Battle of Saragossa* of 1710 during the War of Spanish Succession. This medal depicts Victory laying a shield at the feet of Queen Anne, watched by a standing, helmeted Britannia. Other examples are the oddly eccentric medal of 1711, *The French Lines Passed and Bouchain taken*, on which Britannia, spear and shield resting on a globe supported by a dismantled cannon and cannon balls, sits with her back to the viewer, as a kneeling French officer surrenders his musket and sword. In 1713 the medal marking the Peace of Utrecht has Britannia standing. The events and the medallic response to them did have a bearing on the designs for what were probably pattern coins. The Union of England and Scotland in 1707 produced a pretty reverse of Britannia holding out a joint-stock branch of a conjoined rose and thistle. Another rarity, not employed for currency, was

Above **The French Lines Passed and Bouchain taken**, medal, 1711. John Croker. Silver. British Museum, London. BMG3,EM.262.

Opposite Farthing of Queen Anne, pattern, 1713. John Croker. Copper (enlarged). RMM455.

Below **The Peace of Utrecht**, medal, 1713. John Croker. Gold. British Museum, London. BMG3,EM.41.

the use of the head of the monarch on the reverse as well as the obverse, in which 'heads or tails' were both heads. A 1713 pattern farthing is perhaps the most eccentric of all designs for Britannia: here she sits, rather uncomfortably squeezed into a Classical aedicule or niche. The origin for this unique detail may well have been in the design for the Great Seals of Anne where the Queen sits in state under an arch with Faith and Justice on either side of her.[2] This feature resonates with the carved hoods over outer doors which are so characteristic of the domestic buildings of the period. The counter-seal, or reverse, of the first Great Seal of Anne's reign was equestrian, as was usually the case for counter-seals, and it is surely significant that the Great Seal produced for the Act of Union in 1707 introduces Britannia for the first time, as a symbol of amity, stability and peace. The type reverts to the original design by John Roettiers of the seated Britannia of Charles II, her back to the cliffs and holding an olive branch. Her shield bears the new royal coat of arms for Scotland and England, and a crown hovers over a joint-stock rose and thistle in the field to her right. However, the trials or patterns for the coinage of Anne probably never went into circulation, while what appear to be illicit restrikes circulated 20 or 30 years later.[3] To that extent they are not part of the mainstream, but the ideas were pertinent to the reign.

Queen Anne established a series of thanksgiving services at St Paul's, the first of which celebrated the victory over the French at Blenheim in 1704. St Paul's Cathedral sat in the heart of the City and the commercial world, well removed from the Court and Parliament in Westminster. These thanksgivings were the occasion of splendid and overtly nationalist pageantry. In 1709, two years after the political union of England and Scotland, a warrant for 11 blocks of marble from the royal store at Scotland Yard was addressed to Sir Christopher Wren.[4] This was for a public monument to Queen Anne, to stand at the centre of the enclosure designed by Wren in front of the west front of the Cathedral. It was to be executed by Francis Bird whose workshop had completed the figures in the pediment and the relief over the west door of the Cathedral.[5] The Queen's supporters are four allegorical figures: Britannia, laurel wreathed and carrying a trident, Ireland with her harp, and personifications of France and America. It was the first Baroque monument of its kind in Britain,[6] and in 1712 it put down a royal marker and set a royal presence in the semi-autonomous city state that was the City of London.

51

After 1714, with the arrival and establishment of the Hanoverian dynasty, which from beginning to end met with concerted if intermittent opposition, Britannia fulfilled a role in binding the British Isles into a single identity. George I retained Isaac Newton and John Croker at the Mint, and there were two issues of copper coinage in the reign, one of 1717 and the main one of 1719 to 1724. Numismatists regard these as flawed,[7] probably as a result of experimentation with the alloys on account of the rise in the price of copper, and to technical problems. Britannia on the reverse of the halfpenny and farthing, now in closer fitting drapery, sits on a globe, holding in her right hand a spray of laurel. She carries a spear and her shield bears the crosses of the saints George and Andrew.

It was Queen Caroline, during one of George II's absences, who initiated the coinage of copper in the next reign by a warrant of 1729.[8] Copper coins were still officially understood as mere tokens, 'with us are properly not money … very useful in small home traffic', as the King's Assay Master Joseph Harris put it as late as 1757,[9] and not considered central to the Mint's main business. Nevertheless, counterfeits were ubiquitous, ingenious, and disingenuous:

> It was the common practice of the dealers in this article [counterfeit halfpence and farthings] to fry a pan-full every night after supper for the next day's delivery, thus darkening them, to make them look as if they had been in circulation.[10]

The solution was to stop coining copper altogether in 1754. Thus there were only two distinguishable issues for George II, 1729 to 1739 and 1740 to 1754, using, certainly for the first of these, Croker's original Anne Britannia punch (see Catalogue of Circulating Coins, p. 132).[11]

George III came to the throne in 1760, and although a small issue of farthings was struck using dies of the previous reign, no new copper coin was issued for ten years, and much of what was produced was largely melted down by counterfeiters. The Mint recommended doubling the weight of halfpence and farthings, and patterns were produced in 1788 to designs by Lewis Pingo, Chief Engraver to the Mint. Nothing came of this, and in desperation manufacturers began issuing their own tokens once again, the earliest being issued by the Anglesey Copper Company in 1787. By the 1790s 'evasions', as they were rather charmingly termed, when the design or inscription was slightly altered with the words BRITANNIA'S ISLE, BRITAIN'S ISLES, BRITAIN RULES, and so on, deliberately evaded the law while hoodwinking the illiterate who used them. The designs varied, and many made clear their purpose in their legends: 'for the use of trade', and 'for change not fraud'. They were made in large quantities in Birmingham, thereby gaining that city an unwelcome notoriety for forgery.[12] At this point Matthew Boulton, the industrialist and Fellow of the Royal Society, 'the mere mention of whose name marks an epoch in the art of coining',[13] entered the scene and took coining into the next century.

Above Halfpenny of George III, pattern, 1788. Lewis Pingo. Copper (enlarged). RMM1083.

Chapter 6

Rule, Britannia!

One of the earliest adaptations of the idea of Britannia taken from the coinage was on a door panel for George I's state coach. Painted by James Thornhill in about 1718, it would have had a very high visibility whenever the King moved about London, an event that always attracted a crowd. The image was potent, and was now adopted in the arts for sculpture, specifically monumental and architectural sculpture, and painting and engraving.[1] It appeared both at the high end of the market, in expensive and experimental new materials, and increasingly at the popular end as mass production developed in ceramics, glass and textiles. Jonathan Tyers, the impresario of the pleasure gardens at Vauxhall, commissioned from 1760 to 1764 four vast paintings from Francis Hayman.[2] Two of these were history paintings describing the surrender of Montreal to General Amherst and Lord Clive receiving homage from a Nabob; the other two were allegories of *The Triumph of Britannia* and *Britannia Distributing laurels to the Victorious Generals*.[3] The meaning of this series was not lost on the crowds that swirled past them night after night. The gardens were much frequented by all and sundry: indeed one of their attractions was precisely that there the blurring of social hierarchies could and did happen.[4] People came to see and be seen, and what they saw was further spread abroad by way of prints.

Perhaps most powerful and lasting of all, Britannia appeared in song, famously in the crowd-rousing 'Rule Britannia', in the *Masque of Alfred* by Thomas Arne. *The Seasons* by the Scottish poet James Thomson, first published in 1730, was probably the best-known contemporary British poem of the era. Thomson was a 'resolute economic intergrationalist',[5] a firm believer that England and Scotland united could only be better off economically. His lesser-known poem entitled *Britannia* had been published three years earlier, as a direct attack on Britain's first Prime Minister, Sir Robert Walpole. While *The Seasons* captured the public imagination, it was Thompson's *Britannia* that provided Arne with the words which he set to music for his masque. This was first performed in 1740 for Frederick, Prince of Wales.[6] The words of the penultimate verse read:

> To thee belongs the rural reign;
> Thy cities shall with commerce shine;
> All thine shall be the subject main,
> And every shore it circles thine.

Substitute Frederick for Alfred, the Anglo-Saxon King whose ships kept the Vikings at bay, and translate 'the subject main' as 'seas under British naval control', and the verse encapsulates the mercantile imperialism, which today we might call 'the vision', of the first three Georges. The refrain, known to every child and every reveller in the land, reiterates the patriotic sentiment:

> Rule, Britannia! Britannia, rule the waves:
> Britons never [never never] will be slaves.

One should also bear in mind that Britannia was further identified with principles of liberty based on empiricism, one of the earliest proponents of which was the philosopher John Locke in the late seventeenth century. Locke is regarded as one of the thinkers who ushered in the era of European Enlightenment which dominated the eighteenth century. In his ideas lay the roots of the French Revolution, and they also influenced the founding fathers of the American Constitution. As a member of the Board of Trade, Locke was influential in the development of the North American colonies and wrote a *Treatise on Civil Government* in which he discussed the function of money. Political ideas and ideals ran in parallel with the need for a fiduciary or trustworthy coinage.

In the mid eighteenth century Britannia was a free-floating symbol, one that could be used either by the 'Patriot' or Whig Party, or by the Tory and Jacobite, or 'Country' Party, as well as by mercantilist supporters on both sides of the political spectrum. She could indeed be used within a divided party, as the Whigs often were. Sir Robert Walpole, vilified by his own party, employed both Britannia and Minerva as two independent entities by Michael Rysbrack on the façades of the country house he built at Houghton in Norfolk.[7] As we have seen the neat ambiguity of her alter ego Minerva allows Britannia to be deployed in several guises. In *The Hervey Conversation Piece*, as always with William Hogarth's subject matter, even in a group portrait such as this, there are layers of meaning implied. Minerva here is surely a subliminal Britannia to the first patriot British painter and his subjects, the cohesive coterie of homosexually-inclined Freemasons who

supported Walpole and the Court of Queen Caroline, and George II in absentia.[8] The sitters include John Hervey, Baron Ickworth who commissioned the painting, and on the far right, Thomas Winnington, Lord of the Treasury. In the vast bravura portrait of Colonel William Gordon by Pompeo Batoni, *Roma* is deployed as a Classical prop, but it is not too anachronistic to infer that an associative element is at work. After the failure of the 1745 Jacobite rebellion, only the military could wear the plaid. In wearing the Huntly tartan over the uniform of the Queen's Own Royal Highlanders, the sitter makes a spectacular statement of national identity: a proud Scot under the *Pax Britannica*.[9]

In the complex political associations that surrounded a newly-united country, Frederick, Prince of Wales, the eldest son of George II, was in his own princely Court identified with the Whigs.[10] *The Masque of Alfred* was at the same time expressing Frederick's 'Young Patriots' political opposition both to Sir Robert Walpole, and to the Court of his parents George II and Queen Caroline. A number of medals are evidence of a strongly developed consciousness of national political issues and foreign policy. In particular the medal designed by James Roettiers in 1739 on which a pro-active Britannia, brandishing a sword and inscribed 'I'll avenge my wrongs', is invoked against the Convention of the Prado, a trade treaty deemed detrimental to British interests.[11]

Further, political opposition found symbolic expression in the landscape gardens at Stowe, which had inspired Thomson's *Seasons*, and provided him with his Arcadian setting. These gardens, and their punning Temples of

Above **Britannia**, mid nineteenth century. Staffordshire painted earthenware. Ashmolean Museum, Oxford.
© Ashmolean Museum, University of Oxford HCR7882.

Left **Britannia mourning the death of Frederick, Prince of Wales**, *c.* 1751. St James Factory. Soft paste porcelain. Birmingham Museums and Art Gallery.
© Birmingham Museums Tust 1961.M1.

Liberty, Ancient Virtue, and British Worthies, were set out by Richard Temple, Viscount Cobham, when in opposition to Sir Robert Walpole, with the advice of the great garden designers of the age, Charles Bridgeman (1690–1738) and William Kent.[12] An 'Alto-Relievo of the Four Quarters of the World, bringing their products to *Britannia*' (1738-42) by the Flemish sculptor Peter Scheemakers,[13] was moved in about 1763 from the interior back wall of the Palladian Bridge to the Temple of Concord and Victory, where it was incorporated into the pediment to mark the conclusion of the Seven Years War against the French.[14] This meant trade around the Bay of Mexico and the Caribbean, and into the hinterland of North America along the course of the Mississippi River, came under British control as the French relinquished their hold over Louisiana.

The increase in demand for full-scale figurative funerary monuments in the first half of the eighteenth century, peopled with attributes such as Faith, Fame, Victory and History, did not immediately provide an opportunity for the deployment of Britannia. She does, however, appear mid century as her alias Minerva on a number of monuments such as that to John Campbell, Second Duke of Argyll, by Louis Francois Roubiliac,

Right *Colonel William Gordon*, 1766. Pompeo Batoni. Oil on canvas. The National Trust for Scotland, Fyvie Castle.

completed in 1749,[15] and the monument to Captain Horneck by Peter Scheemakers in Westminster Abbey.[16] The former was a military hero, the latter a military engineer, shown surrounded by his books and compasses. The reference to Britannia is there for all to see, but when Scheemakers redeployed Minerva on the monument to Dr Marmaduke Coghill at Drumcondra in Ireland in 1743,[17] the allusion may be taken as mute, because Ireland had in Hibernia a personification of her own, as can be seen in Michael Rysbrack's monument to Thomas, Baron Wyndham of Finglass, in Salisbury Cathedral.

The earliest example of a funerary monument in an ecclesiastical setting with an allegorical figure which is unquestionably Britannia is to be found on the memorial to Jonas Hanway in Westminster Abbey, designed by John Francis Moore. Here, Britannia appears to be clothing the naked, under the eye of an infant mariner.[18] The philanthropist Hanway was a founder governor of the Foundling Hospital and of the Marine Society, two foundations specifically associated with the needs of the Merchant Marine in its role in establishing the first British Empire.

Left Design for the monument to Jonas Hanway, in the north transept, Westminster Abbey *c.* 1788. John Francis Moore. Pen, ink and watercolour. Victoria & Albert Museum, London. 4910:22.

Since the dissolution of monasteries and convents in the mid sixteenth century, the care of the sick and the poor, and the provision of education itself had become very much the concern of individuals. Many of them maintained or gained anxieties about their immortal souls, and made charitable foundations - schools, hospitals and almshouses - often in their own names, thus also providing themselves with temporal immortality.[19] In the eighteenth century commerce went hand-in-hand with charity, which today would be called philanthropy, and became a mark of social achievement.[20] The Foundling Hospital, which had been granted its charter of incorporation by George II in 1739, was the 'darling project' of Thomas Coram, colonial settler, sea captain, ship builder, merchant and philanthropist.[21] His mission was to highlight the acute social problem of infanticide and child abandonment in London. In this he devoted himself to the establishment of a 'Hospital for the Maintenance and Education of Exposed and Deserted Young Children'.[22] Its purpose was to train rescued boy foundlings for the Navy and Mercantile marine, and to provide trained colonisers, young men and women for an expanding North American empire. The engraver-painter William Hogarth, who was personally involved in the venture, designed the coat of arms, and Britannia appears as a supporter, her lance holding up a Phrygian cap associated with Liberty and Freedom.[23] An inspired and innovative aspect of the foundation, engineered by Hogarth, was that apart from deep-pursed benefactors, artists were included as supporters from its inception.[24] Hogarth, the sculptor Michael Rysbrack, and the architect for the Hospital, Theodore Jacobsen, were the first members of a committee of taste that made it its business to acquire works of art that would attract curious and generous visitors to the Hospital. It became smart to view art, listen to Handel's *Messiah* in the Chapel of a Sunday, and sponsor a child. This link between commerce and charity is well-illustrated in Thomas Bardwell's *Joshua Ward Receiving Money from Britannia, and Bestowing it as Charity on the Needy*. His sitter, Joshua Ward, was a convicted fraudster who made a great deal of money out of quack

medicines known as 'Ward's Pill' and 'Ward's Drops'. He came in for the sharp tongue of Alexander Pope, who was his neighbour in Twickenham:

> He served a 'Prenticeship, who sets up shop;
> Ward try'd on Puppies, and the Poor, his Drop;
> Ev'n Radcliff's Doctors travel first to France,
> Nor dare to practise till they've learned to dance.

The year after this self-promoting portrait was painted, Ward's factory at Twickenham was closed down on account of the pollution it created. Perhaps Ward had hoped that the authoritative figure of Britannia would protect him.[25]

The association of Britannia with trade had been made explicit as early as the mid 1720s in a handsome chimney piece in the City of London. It was commissioned by the East India Company, which had been founded by merchant adventurers under a Royal Charter of Queen Elizabeth I in 1600, for their new 'Office', or London headquarters in Leadenhall Street in 1726.[26] The building was designed by a merchant and amateur architect Theodore Jacobsen, a Master of the London Steelyard, the enclosure and docks on the Thames used for Baltic trade and shipping. The inclusion in chimney pieces of marble reliefs was an innovative import by the Flemish-born sculptor Michael Rysbrack.[27] The iconographic source is to be found in the *Four Continents* by Artus Quellinus on the pediment to the rear elevation of the City Hall in Amsterdam.[28] The relief unambiguously depicted *Britannia receiving the riches of the East Indies*, and would become the prototype for sculptural representation of this type of allegory. Much later, in 1778, the Company commissioned an allegorical ceiling panel, *The East Offering its Riches to Britannia* by Spiridione Roma for the Revenue Committee Room in East India House.[29] A third building designed by Henry Holland and Richard Jupp, and built in 1796-9 for the East India Company at the height of its monopoly, was 'one of the great monuments of the City'.[30] Britannia was

here placed out in the open, isolated above the pediment in a manner that would become prevalent in the next century. She was part of an ambitious group by John Bacon I, which included the King, George III, and Europe and Asia riding respectively a horse and a camel.[31] It was completed by Bacon's son John Bacon II.[32] After the humiliation of the Indian Mutiny in 1857-8, and the subsequent demise of the Company, the building was demolished in 1861, and with it went most of the grandiose work by the Bacons.

John Bacon Senior could justifiably claim to be the first native-born and trained sculptor. One of the first to attend the newly founded Royal Academy Schools, he never made the journey to Rome. He had begun as a commercial modeller for Eleanor Coade, and became her chief designer and modeller in the manufacture of Coadestone. He later worked for both Josiah Wedgwood and Matthew Boulton in the early stages of mass production, a fact that may not have endeared him to his fellow Royal Academicians, most of whom were engaged in distancing themselves from commerce and the applied arts in pursuit of the fine arts of painting in oils and watercolour.

Bacon Senior also provided one of the series of grandiloquent civic memorials in the Guildhall of the City of London, all of them marble paeans to the City's commercial success, and all of them politically-charged. They take their formula entirely from church monuments, particularly those in Westminster Abbey, and most particularly those designed by Louis-François Roubiliac.[33] The first in the series had been a memorial to one of their own, the former Lord Mayor and champion of the City in Parliament, the merchant William Beckford who had died in 1770, in a marble group by John Francis Moore.[34] Next came Bacon's memorial to William Pitt, Earl of Chatham.[35] Pitt the Elder had led the War Party in Parliament, and had always defended the City of London and its liberties, for which he received the Freedom of the City. Commissioned on Pitt's death in 1778 in acknowledgement of this debt, Bacon's memorial is a marvellous late Baroque, pyramidal jumble: four little boys or putti representing the four continents tumble down a vast cornucopia disgorging exotic fruits into the lap of a laconic Britannia, who sits comfortably on a shaggy pet lion. Beside her the figure of the City, identifiable by her mural crown or castellated headdress, reaches up towards Commerce, who sits holding a compass under the protective arm of Pitt. There are naval and mercantile trophies, and a prominent bee skip symbolic of industry, and obliquely the Bank of England. The fulsome inscription on Pitt's memorial is supported by a low-relief roundel, with laurels and a cap of Liberty inscribed LIBERTAS. The commission and the symbolism were a direct challenge to the executive at Westminster, alluding to the failure of the City to win the argument about where Pitt should be buried. The Court of Common Council had petitioned for St Paul's Cathedral to be his burial place, but Westminster Abbey won the honour. And so did Bacon because he was commissioned for the monument in the Abbey too.

The series of memorials or cenotaphs in the Guildhall, having got off to such a spectacular start, continued into the next century. Britannia plays her part, first in the memorial to Horatio, Viscount Nelson who as the inscription avers was 'a man among the few, who appear at different periods to have been created, to promote the grandeur, and add to the security of nations', and continues in adulatory tone and at length in words composed by Richard Brinsley Sheridan.[36] After an open competition in 1806 which produced 27 submissions, including J. C. F. Rossi and Anne Seymour Damer,

the commission was given to the lesser-known sculptor, Rossi's pupil, James Smith. This was indubitably because his proposal, completed by him in 1810, was the cheapest. Smith's Nelson memorial, a much less animated pyramidal composition, is flanked by draped flags, and provides a stage for a suitably hangdog lion on which sits a mourning Britannia holding a relief profile portrait of the dead hero. Britannia's helmeted head rests on her left hand, a pose reminiscent of the Roman 'capta' type and possibly the so-called Penelope type, a figure from a Greek funerary monument. Neptune lolls a little to her right, both poses recalling Michelangelo's *Night* and *Day* on the tomb of Giuliano de Medici in San Lorenzo, Florence. Above them the figure of the City writes down for all to see a list of the great naval engagements that were Nelson's victories. In high relief two handsome, able-bodied, identical-twin seamen, the first of their kind on a memorial, hold attributes of navigation and war. They flank the inscription tablets and a low-relief battle scene, in which ships' mainmasts and spars are shot away, and sails holed.

The third memorial is to William Pitt the Younger by James Bubb another of Rossi's pupils, who appears to have won the competition through malfeasance and the expedient of being again the least expensive proposal.[37] The composition is altogether more symmetrical, and one might say inflexible. Britannia rides a hippocamp or sea horse paddling in the waves. She was holding a thunderbolt 'which she is preparing to hurl against the enemies of her country',[38] an attribute recalling Rubens' Banqueting House ceiling. The restorer reduced the effectiveness of the gesture by replacing the bolt with a fish in her grasp. Above Britannia stand Apollo and Mercury upon a sea-defence wall, derived presumably from prints and possibly casts after the Hadrianic *Apollo Belvedere* and the Florentine cross-legged *Mercury*.[39] Above them stands Pitt in Chancellor of the Exchequer's robes and rhetorical mode 'in the attitude of an Orator'.[40] The work was completed in 1813.

The final memorial in this group may take its composition from that of Beckford's some 40 years earlier. Raised to the Duke of Wellington,[41] it was conceived by the high Victorian sculptor John Bell.[42] With two allegorical figures seated beneath the figure of the commemorated, the spirit and style are, however, very different: there is a muscularity about Peace, her hair undressed, and her companion a very brawny figure of War, his armour relieved by roses, thistles and shamrock, which makes them both more Goth than Classical, more romantic barbarian than vestal virgin, more warrior than legionary. There is no sense of Britannia triumphant here, and it may be a reflection of the new amity between the French and the British that made them allies in the Crimea. There may also be the unspoken understanding in this memorial that with a queen on the throne, in a period of exceptional international peace, and a burgeoning era of public commemoration of individuals, almost exclusively male,[43] the presence of Britannia was not so necessary.

Above Memorial to Arthur Wellesley, Duke of Wellington, 1854. John Bell. Marble. Guildhall, London.

Opposite Memorial to William Pitt the Younger, 1813. James Bubb. Marble (detail). Guildhall, London.

BRITANNIA
BY DIVINE PROVIDENCE
TRIUMPHANT

Scale of Feet

Blake sculp

A Colossal Statue 230 feet high. proposed to be erected on Greenwich hill

Chapter 7

The protecting power or genius of the country

In the late eighteenth century, as in 1672, there was a convergence of international politics, advances in technology, a need for a reform of the coinage, and a shift in style or taste. Two figures now dominate the scene: Matthew Boulton, the industrialist and entrepreneur from Birmingham, and John Flaxman the sculptor, illustrator and designer.[1] Both were leading promoters of the purer Neo-Classical style of the end of the century. Flaxman was the first British sculptor to achieve an international reputation, and had been one of the earliest students admitted, along with John Bacon Senior,[2] to the new Royal Academy Schools in 1769. Like Bacon, and his own favourite pupil and successor E. H. Baily, Flaxman had trained as a modeller and developed and maintained links with manufacturers throughout his working life. Unlike Bacon, however, he spent a number of years working in Rome, and following his experiences there developed a simplicity of form that was far removed from the Baroque grandeur of the Papal City. From 1810 to his death in 1826, he was the first Professor of Sculpture at the Royal Academy Schools.

Flaxman was responsible for adapting Greek and Etruscan vase-painting to the jasperware products of Bentley and Wedgwood's Etruria factory at Burslem in Staffordshire. Painted Greek vases had been brought to England by Sir William Hamilton, 'His Britannick Maiesty's envoy extraordinary' to the Kingdom of the Two Sicilies at Naples,[3] and were sold by him to the British Museum in 1771. They greatly influenced the simplicity of line that gave Flaxman's illustrations to Homer's epics *The Iliad* and *The Odyssey* their particular appeal, one that created Flaxman's international reputation as the 'master of the purist line'.[4] Later, in the Royal Academy Rooms in Somerset House, in a series of professorial lectures Flaxman promoted the work of Antonio Canova, and encouraged an appreciation of the Parthenon Marbles.[5] He appears never to have worked directly on designs for the coinage,[6] but his stylistic influence was immense.

Matthew Boulton built what was at the time the most famous manufacturing business in the world, at Soho, now an inner suburb in the north east of Birmingham. Here later in life Boulton established the first steam-powered mint.[7] He replaced the use of horses with steam power, and harnessed James Watt's steam engine, particularly the rotary motion engine, to drive presses and the machinery for making coin blanks and for striking them. There was a symbiosis of interest here as Boulton and Watt engines had already been introduced to the Cornish copper mining industry, and techniques used in Boulton's button-manufacturing business were adapted for coinage. Boulton was motivated also by a concern for working men who were being cheated by counterfeits in copper,[8] and with a social awareness characteristic of the Enlightenment was asked by Pitt the Younger to come up with ways to eradicate that business. Matthew Boulton

Above Matthew Boulton, *c.* 1815.
John Flaxman. Marble. Soho House,
Birmingham Museum & Art Gallery.
© Birmingham Museums Tust 1995p9.

Opposite A Colossal Statue 230 feet high: proposed to be erected on Greenwich hill, 1799.
William Blake after John Flaxman. Etching.
British Museum, London. 1894,0612.35.1.

invested heavily in technology and design in the battle against counterfeiters. One of his solutions was to introduce the *incusa*, lettering on the rim. Another, involving many experiments, was the invention of a retaining collar to ensure a constant diameter and give uniformity to the edges of blanks in the striking process. James Watt declared in a memorandum on Boulton's death:

> Had Mr. B done nothing more in the world than what he has done in improving the coinage, his fame would have deserved to be immortalised; and if it is considered that this was done in the midst of various other important avocations, & at an enormous expense for which he could have no certainty of an adequate return, we shall be at a loss as to whether to admire most his ingenuity, his perseverance or his munificence.[9]

In 1786 Boulton supplied 100 tons of copper coinage to the East India Company, for Sumatra,[10] and in 1787 the Anglesey Copper Mines Company issued full weight penny and halfpenny tokens minted at Soho. In 1792 it was the ironworks at Coalbrookdale, and the following year the iron-master John Wilkinson in Birmingham, who turned to Boulton for tokens. These were issued to pay the wages of a newly industrialised class, and while providing the small change for daily needs, tokens acted too as advertisements for successful companies.[11] Clearly government was failing in its fiscal responsibilities to provide copper coinage. A Committee of the Privy Council was set up to consider reform of the coinage in 1787, and the following year the 'London' or as Boulton termed it the 'England', or 'Royal' Mint sought designs from its own engravers for a new coinage. The reform process was beset by procrastination, but Boulton continued to build the presses that he foresaw would be needed, and to strike the copper tokens that the new industries required. It remained Boulton's ambition to provide the nation's official coinage.

In 1797 Boulton won the government contract, when the nation, deeply engaged in war with France, required a large supply of copper currency. Once again advances in technology and cost-effectiveness coincided with a change of pattern or design, and Britannia appeared on the newly-introduced copper penny and twopence. Boulton, the entrepreneur whose business it was to make and sell desirable things, known then as 'toys', but today as luxury goods, was fully aware of the importance of good design. In 'bringing to perfection the art of coining',[12] he invited a number of foreign engravers to Soho, among them the Swiss Jean-Pierre Droz who had worked at the Paris Mint on the Napoleonic coinage. In 1788 Droz offered an entirely nude Britannia in a trial for the reverse of the halfpenny. He was in competition with Lewis Pingo, Chief Engraver to the Mint, who provided an innovative standing Britannia for pattern halfpennies and farthings of the size of pennies and halfpennies with which they have been confused.[13] The Droz version was emphatically better modelled than Pingo's rather limp Britannia, but the government procrastinated, and Droz stayed only until 1791.

Boulton had better luck with the Flemish die-cutter Conrad Heinrich Küchler, who was to work at Soho from 1793 to 1810.[14] Küchler's design reverted to the Roman seated Britannia. Its gentle waves, a ship on the horizon and, for the first time, the introduction of a trident in place of a lance, were all reminders of Britannia's nautical and maritime significance. This design would remain the formula for the most recognisable Britannia type on the coinage to the present day.[15] At the time Sir George Yonge, Master of the Mint, supported his Chief Engraver Lewis Pingo's design, and later advised him on the appearance of a Minerva-like helmet, which would subsequently become ubiquitous.[16] In 1797, however, the Privy Council Committee on Coin was looking at a design by Nathaniel Dance-Holland, brother-in-law of the Chairman of the Committee, Lord Liverpool. Proposed on 14 March, it seems it was presented to George III on 28 March:

> ... a beautiful Drawing presented to this Committee by Nathaniel Dance Esquire M.P. wherein Britannia is presented as sitting upon a Rock in the midst of the Ocean, holding a Trident in her Left Hand instead of a Spear; and a Branch of Olive, the Emblem of peace, in her Right Hand; with the Dates inscribed on a Rock of Three memorable Naval Victories obtained over your Majesty's Enemies in the present War – vizt.- June 1st June 23d. and February 14th.[17]

The King approved the design for the penny on 1 June. It must be assumed that the design by Dance-Holland was sent to Birmingham to be worked on by Küchler, for the Committee decided in favour of Boulton's 'cartwheel' type for the one and two penny pieces. These were large and heavy, more like medals than coins, and were called 'cartwheels' because of the wide raised rim, designed to protect the image from wear. In 1810 the rebuilt Royal Mint on Tower Hill opened, and the new coining presses developed, and now supplied, by Boulton would remain in use there until the 1880s.

Below Penny of George III, pattern, 1797. Conrad Heinrich Küchler. Copper (enlarged). RMM1096.

Matthew Boulton was a close friend and business-associate of Josiah Wedgwood. They were both leading members of the Lunar Society, that influential group of Midlands amateurs, 'fathers of the industrial revolution', that had the newly-industrialised Birmingham as its epicentre.[18] The Society was so called because its members would walk or ride at the full moon to attend gatherings. It is not mere conjecture to suppose that design was part of the currency of conversation between the two men. In 1787 *Mercury uniting the hands of Britain and France* was commissioned by Wedgwood from John Flaxman, to celebrate the Anglo-French Commercial Treaty of 1786, to be made in Wedgwood's new Jasperware.[19] Wedgwood wrote to Flaxman:

> We must take care not to shew that these representations were invented by an Englishman: as they are meant to be conciliatory, they should be scrupulously impartial. The figures…should be equally magnificent & important, in their dress, attitude, character and attributes: and Mercury should not perhaps seem more inclined to one than the other…and if you think there is no impropriety in it, I should wish France to have her helmet & shield as well as Britannia, and the Fleur de lis upon the latter.[20]

The plaque appeared in Wedgwood's French catalogue in 1788, the year the Committee was considering patterns from both the Mint and from Boulton.

Above **Mercury uniting the hands of Britain and France**, 1787. John Flaxman. Jasperware. Wedgwood Museum, Barlaston, Stoke-on-Trent. ©Wedgwood Museum / WWRD 9473.

Opposite **Britannia Triumphant**, c. 1800. William Hackwood after Henry Webber. Jasperware. Modern replica. Wedgwood Museum, Barlaston, Stoke-on-Trent. This virtuoso piece had pride of place in Wedgwood's new showrooms in York Street, St James' and can been seen in the print in Ackerman's *Repository of the Arts*, 1809. ©Wedgwood Museum / WWRD 9551.

A monument in Westminster Abbey to Captains Bayne, Blair and Manners, who had been killed in a naval engagement in 1782, was designed by Joseph Nollekens, and paid for by George III and Parliament. In the ten years that lapsed between commission and execution, the Baroque configuration of the original design gave way to the purer Neo-Classical style in the completed monument.[21] It is indicative of the shift in taste, whereby the influence of Rome and Roman antiquities was superseded by Greece. The writings of, among others, the French engraver Charles Nicolas Cochin and Johann Joachim Winckelmann, whose *Geschichte der Kunst des Alterthums* (History of Ancient Art), was the earliest analysis of Greek and Roman art when published in 1764, were highly influential. These two were among the first to perceive that much Roman art, and specifically sculpture, was derivative of Greek art, and turned their eyes towards Greece, in a swing of the aesthetic pendulum from which emerged the pan-European style of Neo-Classicism. This was espoused by, among many others, the Scottish architect Robert Adam,[22] while artists and sculptors such as John Flaxman came to pursue the 'true simple antique style' of Greece.

Right **Minerva Gustiniani**, Roman copy of a Greek sculpture, late fifth/early fourth century BC. Marble. Vatican Museum, Rome.
© PhotoBliss / Alamy Stock Photo.

A possible early source for this shift in aesthetic understanding may be the Minerva Gustiniani now in the Vatican Museum, excavated in 1631.[23] This was not copied until towards the end of the eighteenth century when it came to be admired as an example of the 'high austere', specifically Greek, style, the closest to Phidias' Athene for the Parthenon. It was engraved by Nathaniel Marchant, Assistant Engraver to the Mint from 1797 to 1815,[24] on a sardonyx intaglio for Charles Long, President of the Committee for the Inspection of National Monuments. As the need for memorials to the fallen grew, this committee had been set up to supervise the commissioning of numerous monuments to the heroes of the Napoleonic Wars. Among them was the monument to Admiral Lord Nelson in the south transept of St Paul's Cathedral, for which Flaxman adopted the Minerva type. The source was not lost on a contemporary German visitor, Ludwig Schorn, who described the monument thus:

> the artist has made as evident as possible the purity of his purpose shaped by antiquity, and the nobility of forms which he learnt from there... Britannia, a tall figure similar to the war-like Minerva is leading two young mariners.[25]

Left Monument to Horatio, Viscount Nelson, 1807-8. John Flaxman. Marble. St Paul's Cathedral. © akg-images / Bildarchiv Monheim / Florian Monheim / Roman von Götz.

Modern commentators have avoided the allusion to Britannia, preferring to see the standing female figure as Minerva in 'a less stridently didactic and patriotic role'.[26]

The iconography of Britannia flourished in the Napoleonic Wars as part of the polemic and propaganda against Napoleon, the bogey 'Boney', and the age-old enemy the French. In the popular imagery of political cartoons by James Gillray, George Cruikshank and Thomas Rowlandson, Britannia was such a recurrent image that the subject deserves a book on its own, but an example must suffice here. In popular art, such as prints and glass paintings, some of which combined both print and paint on glass, Britannia became wholly identified with national endeavour. The Trafalgar Vase, designed by Flaxman, and made by the royal goldsmiths Rundell, Bridge and Rundell, has a cast and applied figure of a seated Britannia. More than 60 of these were made for presentation to naval and military officers by Lloyd's Patriotic Fund. To mark British naval victories over the French in 1799, Flaxman designed proposals for a number of public monuments.[27] In his pamphlet, *Letter to the Committee for Raising the Naval Pillar under the Patronage of his Royal Highness the Duke of Clarence,* for which William Blake did the

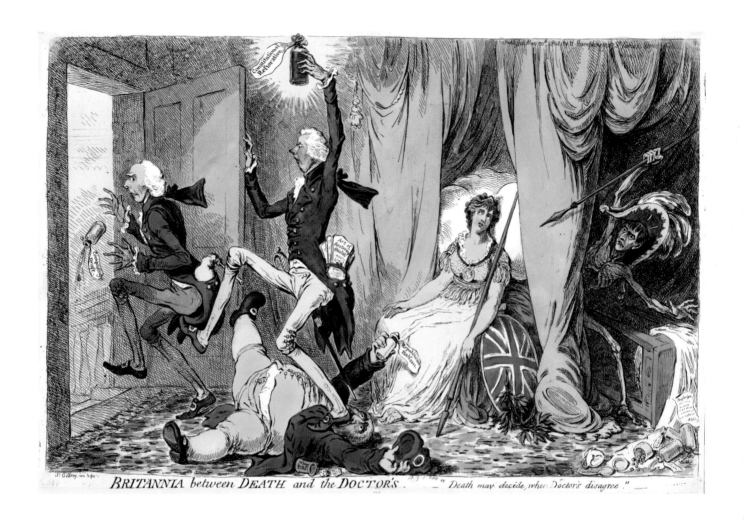

BRITANNIA between DEATH and the DOCTOR'S. ——"Death may decide, when Doctor's disagree."

engravings, Flaxman cited precedents from the ancient world, and espoused the cause of the public statue. Had any of Flaxman's ideas been executed they would have been colossal: the standing figure of Britannia on Greenwich Hill, for example, would have been 230 feet high, a considerable feat of engineering. As Flaxman observed:

> How much more sentiment and interest there is in a fine human figure than can possibly be produced in the choicest piece of architecture, and especially when the figure represents the protecting power or genius of the country.[28]

Chapter 8

Una guides the British Lion

Flaxman's final project in 1825 was the scheme for the architectural sculpture on the grandiose triumphal arch designed by John Nash to commemorate the end of the Napoleonic Wars. Originally intended as a gateway to Buckingham Palace, Nash had decreed that the figures should 'manifest the Gusto Greco'.[1] A model was made in Flaxman's workshops that included the superstructure for a proposed equestrian statue of George IV.[2] Below it, above an attic storey resting on the arch, sat on one side Europe and Asia, and on the other Britannia holding a trident in her right hand, and in her left in place of her shield a relief medallion with the portrait of Nelson. Flaxman died that year, and his work was continued by E. H. Baily, Richard Westmacott, and J. C. F. Rossi. Baily was to carve Britannia, the portrait of Nelson and the lion and the unicorn, among other subjects. Sir Francis Chantrey was persuaded to carry out the equestrian statue on condition that it was made in bronze.[3] On the death of George IV in 1830 and the appointment of Edward Blore, as architect in place of Nash, the arch was dismantled. Blore went on to become an early exponent of the Gothic Revival, as in his Choir Screen in Westminster Abbey of 1838. Most of the sculpture was, however, complete and was accommodated elsewhere at Buckingham Palace, and on the façade of the new National Gallery.[4] This, a cultural response to the Louvre and, with the British Museum, to the Musée Napoleon, was under construction to the designs of William Wilkins between 1833 and 1838. Britannia, her trident replaced with a lance, was now installed as Minerva on the end of the East Wing of the Gallery. She marks the entrance to what was originally the Royal Academy, which moved from its rooms in Somerset House to share the building with the National Gallery in 1838. She remains largely unnoticed under a fine London plane tree, above the entrance to a café. At the same time, 200 yards away on the corner of Pall Mall and Waterloo Place, the intellectually exclusive club, the Athenaeum, whose first Secretary was the scientist Michael Faraday, had been built to designs by the Greek Revival architect, Decimus Burton. The figure on the portico is a gilded copy by Edward Hodges Baily of the *Pallas Athene of Velletri*.[5] Given that this newly redeveloped quarter of London from Trafalgar Square and the National Gallery to the clubs on Pall Mall was an architectural paean to British supremacy in the Napoleonic Wars, Britannia and Minerva once again coalesced. At the same time the three institutions, the National Gallery, the Royal Academy, and the Athenaeum, represented aspects of Britain's cultural and intellectual establishment. Politicians and members of the armed forces met elsewhere.

The politicians' meeting place, the Houses of Parliament, was in the process of being transformed by Charles Barry and A. W. N. Pugin into a vast Gothic palace after the fire of 1834 had destroyed most of its original buildings. The Gothic Revival of the second quarter of the nineteenth century, the dramatic stylistic change that most obviously in architecture

Above **Pallas Athene**, *c.* 1830. Edward Hodges Baily. Gilded metal. Athenaeum, Waterloo Place, London.

Opposite **Model for gateway to Buckingham Palace**, 1825. John Flaxman. Plaster. Victoria & Amp; Albert Museum, London. A.14-1939.

loosened the grip of the Classical on the visual arts, had at first glance little or no impact on the overall design of the coinage. A contemporary commentator declared:

> In 1825, when engaged by the directions of the then Master of the Mint, Mr (afterwards Lord) Wallace, in bringing out a complete set of the coins of George the Fourth, William Wyon designed a new Britannia, than which there is not a single figure more classical, simple, and beautiful on any Greek or Roman coin that I am acquainted with. She sits on a rock, looking to her left, armed as Minerva; drapery close, and sweetly arranged, arms unclothed, the right resting on the upper part of the shield, the left upholding the trident, the hand very gracefully turning inwards. In the exergue the rose, thistle and shamrock combined.[6]

William Wellesley Pole, an elder brother of the Duke of Wellington, became in 1814 Master of the Mint. He was to set about a reform of the currency and its design. Pole found in Benedetto Pistrucci,[7] an Italian gem engraver, a designer to fulfil his ambition for the coinage. Encouraged by W. R. Hamilton to come to London from Rome in 1815, Pistrucci was to design the new gold sovereign of George III. For the reverse he produced one of the finest designs in the history of British coinage, the St George and the dragon of 1817.[8] This certainly owed a debt to the cavalcade of horsemen in low relief on the Parthenon marbles, for which W. R. Hamilton, when Lord Elgin's secretary, had been a most persuasive advocate.[9] Pistrucci's design for the reverse of the sovereign was adapted for the silver crown the following year. Apart from Britannia it was the first time a non-heraldic image had appeared on the coinage for 150 years.[10]

The first copper coins struck at the new Mint on Tower Hill in 1821 were farthings made from melted down halfpennies from the old Mint. Britannia now faced east on the coin, towards Europe, where before she had always faced west, towards the Americas. This may be tacit acceptance of the loss of her first empire, and the importance of Britain's role in Europe in the first decades of the nineteenth century. She wears her newly-acquired helmet, but the ship has disappeared, while a lion's head appears at her feet. The coin was not, however, a success, largely because the King disliked his portrait on the obverse, and Pistrucci refused to work from an approved image, the bust of George IV by Sir Francis Chantrey. Instead the work was given to William Wyon.[11]

The internal politics of the Mint were complex, and the intensity of the rivalry between Pistrucci and Wyon within the institution was such that it may have affected any serious consideration of innovation in the lower denominations. Across three changes of succession from George III, George IV and William IV to Victoria, the detail on the reverse varies sometimes minutely, but the overall formula and choice of attributes remains much the same: a twitch of the drapery, a sandal strap, waves, a ship on the horizon, a laurel wreath, and sprigs of patriotic flowers in the exergue, which since the Union with Ireland in 1801 included a shamrock. From 1839 to 1860 the trident on Wyon's reverse for the Victoria penny is variously ornamented, with the exception of the years 1853 to 1857 when it is plain.[12] These details, far from mere tweaks for a numismatist, are essential in differentiating successive dies, while retaining the essence of Britannia for the people on the street. As one distinguished numismatist put it, the Britannia reverse designed by William Wyon for George IV, William IV and Victoria 'reached its zenith in the perfect balance of its composition'.[13]

BY J. P. DROZ, 1788.

BY W. WYON, R.A. 1825.

THE BRITANNIAS OF DROZ AND WYON

INSULATED AS ON THE COINAGE OF

M. BOULTON. A.D. 1797.

DRAWN BY W. L. CASEY, SCHOOL OF DESIGN, CORK, 1852.

BARCLAY, S.C. GERRARD ST LONDON.

Top Obverse of the Coronation medal of Queen Victoria, 1838. Benedetto Pistrucci. Gold. RMM23,024.

Above Penny postage stamp of Victoria, the Penny Black, 1840. William Wyon. The Postal Museum, London.

Below Five-sovereign piece of Victoria, Una guiding the British Lion, 1839. William Wyon. Gold (enlarged). RMM3716.

Pistrucci's Coronation medal of 1838 presents the new Queen as a Canovaesque 'Ideal Beauty', complete with diadem, her hair prettily bound up in a *sakkoi* or hair net.[14] As late as 1840, Wyon's essentially Classical and popular design provided the image for the 'Penny Black' on the introduction of the uniform postal rate.[15] However, W. R. Hamilton's polemic on the choice of the Gothic over the 'Greek style' for the Houses of Parliament, 'On the Propriety of adopting the Greek style of architecture in preference to the Gothic, in the construction of the new Houses of Parliament', in 1836 may be seen as a rearguard action on behalf of the Classicists.

Nevertheless, there are two examples in the coinage that subtly reflect the emergent change. Both are by the newly-designated Chief Engraver to the Mint, William Wyon, a member of a generations-old dynasty of medallists and die engravers of possible Flemish antecedence: Willliam's grandfather George, an immigrant from Cologne, had worked for Matthew Boulton at Soho in Birmingham.[16] The first change in the imagery on the coinage represents the political and philosophical shift away from the Classical world of Greece and Rome towards native British roots. This was not a new identification, having been an ingredient of Whig 'patriotism' since the 1730s.[17] Wyon's design Una guiding the British Lion for the reverse of the pattern five-sovereign gold coin of 1839,[18] was an overt compliment to the new Queen, Victoria. In a many-layered symbolism, she was no longer a Greek goddess, but instead the muse was Celtic: she could be the Una of Irish mythology, either the fairy queen wife of Finn Bheara, King of the Galway Fairies, or of the giant Finn McCool, or she could be the later Una of Edmund Spenser's *Faerie Queene*. In this profoundly allegorical and

courtly epic addressed to Queen Elizabeth I, 'Gloriana', Una represents Truth, 'the One and Only', the one true Protestant church. Una could be both feisty and unwavering: as she appears on Wyon's coin, her hair is plaited in the manner of northern European tradition, and she wears a cloak and gown in a medieval style recalling Walter Scott's novel *Ivanhoe* (1820), and the pseudo-chivalric Eglinton Tournament of 1839, the lodestone of the change in taste and style of the time.[19] As Queen, Una wears a crown, and carries an orb and sceptre, and would fleetingly appear again on the reverse of a pattern penny in 1859.[20] The image of a woman on the throne merges, in Una, with that of the mythic or allegorical, a metamorphosis which also extended to Britannia, the image associated with national identity. This usage became more compelling as Victoria's long reign stretched on. Among William Wyon's many other contributions to the medallic arts was the design for the silver crown of 1847. Described as a 'Gothic' head,[21] it depicts the Queen, not just head but bust, wearing the Imperial State Crown. Her hair is braided into loops in a manner significant of pre-Classical Britain, and she wears what may be a cope-like cape with an embroidered plastron border implying a semi-sacerdotal persona. The inscription is in a Gothic face.

In November 1859 William's son Leonard recorded in his diary that he was working on a model for the portrait of the Queen 'with lengthened bust'. However, royal objections to the portrait, which was intended to replace the 'Young Head', and to age the Queen gracefully, held up the process. Meanwhile, William Gladstone as Chancellor of the Exchequer had intimated that Wyon's Britannia was to be used for the reverse of the penny, halfpenny and farthing of a new bronze issue.[22] This was the occasion when for the first time a lighthouse, supposedly the Eddystone,[23] was introduced, a symbol of the sea and of feats of engineering, and by inference of Britain's mastery of both. The decision to convert the coinage from copper to bronze was officially announced in August 1859, with the main contract going to Messrs James Watt, to strike under Mint supervision the huge quantities now necessary.[24] Wyon went twice in December 1859 to Osborne House on the Isle of Wight, 'on the subject of the new bronze coinage', where the Queen 'sat, or rather stood, to me'.[25] This may be an indication that Victoria did indeed see herself as the embodiment of Britannia.[26] On the second visit, she and Prince Albert 'expressed themselves much pleased. The Queen gave me a photograph of herself'.[27] Finally, Wyon was able to record in his diary that he had been to the Mint to see the pence and halfpence 'struck well from the new dies', and concluded, clearly with some relief, that, 'I trust [this] will complete all that I have to do with the coinage'.[28] Wyon's coin became known as the 'Bun Penny', from the Queen's hair being dressed in a bun. It remained in circulation as legal tender for 100 years, well into the 1960s.[29]

In 1893 the third issue of the reign provided a final portrait of the ageing Queen, although the bronze coins were not changed until 1895. The obverse of the penny, halfpenny and farthing carried a veiled head engraved by G. W. De Saulles after a model by Thomas Brock, while the reverse image of Britannia was copied by De Saulles, with modifications, from Leonard Wyon. De Saulles omitted the lighthouse and the ship, while the figure of Britannia with a larger, more oval shield, became more vigorous and upright.[30] As Charles Peck put it in 1960, 'with this issue the figure of Britannia assumed the form and style which was to remain essentially the same up to the present'.[31]

Above Penny of Victoria, 1860. Leonard Wyon. Bronze. RMM4228.

Below Penny of Victoria, 1895. G. W. De Saulles, portrait after Thomas Brock. Bronze. RMM8048.

Chapter 9
Looking at an image of Victoria

....

The failure of the East India Company to manage its own affairs, symbolised by the trial of Warren Hastings from 1784 to 1795, had coincided with the loss of the first British Empire in North America.[1] This coincidence turned Britain's interests, both political and commercial, away from the Atlantic and towards the Indian sub-continent.[2] The business of the East India Company was to have an increasing impact on government and statecraft, until, after the Indian Mutiny in 1857 at the height of Victoria's reign, any semblance of power was finally removed from the Company, and India itself became central to matters of state in foreign affairs, governance and commerce. The transfer of India to direct government rule prompted a replacement of the Company's coinage by a new set of designs, which the Royal Mint was authorised by the Treasury to produce in 1859.[3] Leonard Wyon recorded that he was working on designs for the Indian coinage, which meant several sketching trips to the East India Company Museum in Leadenhall Street.[4] His design for the portrait on the rupee and anna relied heavily on his father William Wyon's earlier 'Gothic' version of 1846, although now the Queen wears an embroidered kurta, or raja's coat, with a string of pearls at her throat.[5] At the same time he worked with the Bank of England on the design of the Indian banknote.[6]

A significant aspect of colonialism was that it generated early visual representations of the peoples of the Empire in non-European, possibly 'native' dress, whether in Canada or India. One of the earliest engraved images of Britannia associated with India is the vignette on a map of the sub-continent entitled *Hindoostan*, of 1782-5, in which a helmeted, Minerva-like figure, her lance resting on her left shoulder, exchanges documents – maps for sacred texts – with a group of Hindu pundits wearing *doti*. They are observed by a cartographer of the East India Company, and an official or a sepoy in a turban.[7] In Exeter Cathedral, standing equal to a British soldier in high relief, a member of one of the First Nation tribes of Ontario appears as a warrior, his hair caught up in a top-knot, on the monument by John Flaxman to Lt Gen. John Simcoe, founder of Toronto.[8] This may have been an early manifestation of the paternalistic ethos of the 'noble Savage',[9] or, in keeping with Neo-Classicism, was intended to resonate with minimally-clad Greek warriors. In 1814 Thomas Wyon, another member of this extended family, designed the medal for the Indian Chiefs of Canada, in which a seated Britannia, his first attempt at the reverse, presented 'an Indian of a fine athletic figure, in proper costume' with a medal.[10]

Respect and admiration for native traditions and local cultural norms had been expressed at its earliest in south India by the seventeenth-century Italian Jesuit missionary Roberto de Nobili.[11] This way of thinking was to play a part in the evolution of the coinage, and the numismatist,

....

Opposite Queen Victoria Memorial, 1903-24. Sir Thomas Brock. Marble and bronze. The Mall, London.
© QEDimages / Alamy Stock Photo.

Below Gothic Crown, 1847. William Wyon. Silver. RMM3882.

Bottom Rupee, 1861. Leonard Wyon. Copper. RMM9724

Below *Indian Chiefs of Canada*,
1814. Thomas Wyon. Bronze.
Plate from Richard Sainthill,
*An Olla Podrida or Scraps,
Numismatic, Antiquarian and
Literary*, vol. II, London 1853,
(enlarged). RMM.

antiquarian, and *eminence grise* at the Mint Richard Sainthill was quite clear about it in his book *Olla Podrida*. In the chapter entitled 'Objections to English Inscriptions on the Coinage of the Honourable the East India Company',[12] he gathered a number of his published 'remarks', in which he expressed his view that when in India do as Indians do, be they Muslim, Hindu, Sikh or Jain. He suggested the establishment of a school of engravers native to the sub-continent, and in a subsequent chapter went further in suggesting that a depiction of Vishnu bursting from a tree to destroy a giant be adopted as the design for the reverse of medals awarded to Indian soldiers.[13] Sainthill went so far as to say to Wyon:

> I suggest to you that, instead of employing the Gods of Greece*
> and Rome, and the personifications of Christianity paganized, you
> will do much better to make the medal *Indian* in its subjects and
> language.
> *Mars, Minerva, Britannia, and so forth – nonentities.[14]

Whatever the motive, it was his hope to 'Indianize an Indian medal of merit'.[15]

To paraphrase Sir Roy Strong when writing of Queen Elizabeth I, 'to all intents and purposes looking at an image of [Victoria] was looking at an image of [Britannia]'.[16] In India this, as recent scholarship has made clear, is how the two images were received, two sides of the same coin so to speak,[17] although Britannia herself did not appear on Indian coinage, just as she was absent from coins for other dominions and colonies. A lithograph published in Kolkata in 1878 graphically makes the point. It depicts an old and frail Mother India, the *Bharat Mata*, presenting a boy foundling, an infant India, to a more than usually motherly Britannia with her shield and lance. Britannia is wearing a string of pearls and a crown – Victoria's Imperial Crown – as they appear on Leonard Wyon's portrait, adapted for the obverse of the *rupee* and *anna* of 1861. Here, on a street poster, is Britannia unequivocally the veiled Queen Empress.[19]

From 1828 the Scottish Institution and the Scottish Academy in Edinburgh were housed in the same building designed by William Playfair. The seated figure of Queen Victoria, draped as though she were Britannia,[20] looks down from the low portico pediment on Princes Street. Completed in 1843, this is indubitably an overt compliment to the new Queen by the young and ambitious sculptor John Steell. Nevertheless, it was not his first thought, as a presentation elevation by Playfair of 1832 shows the original intention was to make Minerva the pedimental figure.[21] The RSA pediment was the first of Steell's many public statues, and the first of Victoria as Queen. Soon after, Steell became Sculptor-in-Ordinary to Her Majesty in Scotland, and the Academy was given a Royal Charter and became the Royal Scottish Academy.[22]

On the death of Prince Albert in 1861 the Lord Mayor of London called a public meeting inviting subscriptions for a monument to his memory. Queen Victoria set up an advisory committee to the same end. George Gilbert Scott's Gothic design for the Albert Memorial, which took its inspiration from the fourteenth-century Eleanor Crosses, was accepted by the Queen in 1863, and the monument was finally completed in 1876, when the colossal gilded figure of the prince was set in place. Here, among many figures and groups, Britannia takes her seat in an equality of nations, with Germany, France and Italy below Europa on her legendary bull, in a marble group by Patrick MacDowell. Only the trident and the waves lapping the edge of the plinth distinguished her from these other generic types.[23] The purpose of the monument as an apotheosis of the Queen's consort demanded a sublimation of Britannia, and with her any suggestion of the Queen herself.

The statue of Queen Victoria outside Kensington Palace was designed and executed by her fourth daughter, the sculptress Princess Louise, Duchess of Argyll. Presented by the Kensington Golden Jubilee Memorial Executive Committee in 1893, it was purposefully anachronistic in depicting the Queen in Coronation robes at the age of 19. Victoria had been born at Kensington Palace, and when not at Claremont, Esher, had grown up there, until summoned from her bed in the Palace to become Queen in 1837. The image may have found its inspiration in a portrait of the young Queen in Coronation robes by Sir George Hayter.[24] One might easily be forgiven for taking her for Britannia, the angle of the seated figure and the position of the legs, one knee forward, one back, clearly recalls the earliest Britannia of 1672. Perhaps this is just a traditional sculptural design for a seated monarch, but it may be that the image had been so absorbed into the nation's subconscious that it was now impossible to disassociate from this interpretation. A version was raised in Montreal in 1895 outside the Royal Victoria College for Higher Education for Women.[25]

If Princess Louise's image of her mother as a young Queen has subliminal undertones of a Britannia figure, the Victoria Memorial by Sir Thomas Brock installed outside Buckingham Palace converts the monarch into a matronly Britannia, the mother of her people. When Victoria died in 1901, the second British Empire, though not yet at its fullest extent, was certainly at its apogee. At the end of her long reign, 63 years on the throne, Victoria was again to be the subject of a memorial. However, as contemporary commentators made clear this was to be not just another memorial to add to the 84 extant at her death,[26] but to be the mother of all memorials. Designed by Sir Aston Webb in 1903, the group has a rich supply of sculpture by Sir Thomas Brock, 'the great plagiarist of the New Sculpture',[27] in two types of marble and bronze. A number of allegorical figures congregate around the Queen Empress, seated on a Renaissance throne: among them are Motherhood, Manufacture, Peace and Progress. These epitomise the Pax Britannica, but in the presence of the Queen, Britannia herself is absent. Begun in 1906 and unveiled in 1911, the Victoria Memorial was not completed until 1924.[28]

The memorial looks down Aston Webb's Mall to Admiralty Arch, the nearest thing to an imperial avenue that London has. An integral part of Empire image-making, the *rond-point* or circus, itself a large traffic roundabout, on which the memorial stands, remains part of ceremonial activity on the Mall.[29] The extended ceremonial route from Buckingham Palace passes under Admiralty Arch, across the south-east corner of Trafalgar Square, past Nelson's Column and Hubert Le Sueur's equestrian Charles I, with Whitehall, the centre of imperial administration, and the not-so-old Gothic clock-tower of Big Ben and St Stephen's Tower visible to the right, along the Strand, past the Law Courts through what was the heart of the newspaper industry in Fleet Street to St Paul's Cathedral. It ends at the feet of the statue of Queen Anne. From one great Queen to another, the symbolic association of these two female monarchs with Britannia was more than subliminal: it was surely meant.

Chapter 10

An unembarrassed fervour for King and country

In 1901 the death of Queen Victoria was marked at Esher, the Surrey town where she had spent most of her childhood, with a monument that included a life-size bronze standing figure of Britannia. Two years later the British Numismatic Society adopted as its seal a standing Britannia. Meanwhile, increasing dissatisfaction was expressed with the artistic merits of the coinage. In an article on 'The New Coinage' in the *Art Journal* for March 1893, the painter Philip Wilson Steer described it as 'the apotheosis of machinery and the almost extinction of Art'.[1] This refrain had been heard before, and would be heard regularly throughout the new century. The reworking of Wyon's 1860 Britannia in 1895 incurred ridicule in *Punch*:

> Britons good at making money,
> Cannot make a coin that's decent.
> Rule Britannia? Rot sophistic!
> Had I really sway I'd rule
> No more duffers inartistic
> With my coins should play the fool.[2]

The accession of Edward VII in 1901 led to an immediate decision by the Mint authorities for a new look to the coinage, the copper and bronze having remained almost static across the 60 years of Victoria's reign, notably in Leonard Wyon's design for the so-called 'Bun' penny of 1860. While the Wyon-inspired figure of Britannia on the reverse of the penny, halfpenny and farthing remained the same, G. W. De Saulles was instructed in that year to replace the heraldic devices on the reverse of the silver florin or two-shilling piece with another Britannia, to distinguish it from the half-crown. George William De Saulles had attended Birmingham School of Art and served his apprenticeship with the Birmingham die-sinker John Wilcox. A prolific and inventive medallic engraver, he was in effect 'head-hunted' by the Mint.[3] It was said that the art of coin-engraving before he was appointed to the Mint had died out.[4] Thereafter, from 1893 to his early death in 1903, his designs, though not always popular, were impressive and his coins and medals as significant in the twentieth century as the Wyons' had been in the nineteenth. De Saulles produced the design for a standing Britannia for the British trade-dollar for Hong Kong, by now the third most important port in the Empire, and the Far East, of which 270 million pieces were made from 1895 to 1935.[5] This was in competition with the highly successful Mexican dollar as a trade coin, and had to convince of its authority in very different fiscal cultures. A portrait of Queen Victoria was not used for fear that at 75 she should die, and any change would undermine the stability needed to

Above Seal of the British Numismatic Society, 1903, designed by senior officers of the Society based on a mid eighteenth-century medal. RMM.

Opposite Florin of Edward VII, electrotype, 1902. G. W. De Saulles. Nickel-faced copper. RMM.

impress the Chinese. Britannia was chosen for the obverse as an easily recognisable symbol of the British Empire that was acceptable to all.[6] De Saulles' model was the 17-year-old Susan Hicks Beach, the daughter of Sir Michael Hicks Beach, Chancellor of the Exchequer and Master of the Mint.[7] Then in 1900 De Saulles designed the Queen's South Africa Medal, on which Britannia gestures encouragingly to the troops, in a manner much closer to the treatment of La France, Marianne, who is usually seen in action, and often on the offensive. For the new coinage of Edward VII in 1901, De Saulles' model was once again Susan Hicks Beach. This prompted a question in the House of Commons from Ellis Griffith as to the design of the new florin, and whether there had been an open competition, something which would become increasingly an issue as the century progressed. Griffith further criticised the design: the horizon sloped left to right, the figure and head were not in proportion, there was no indication of a second foot, there was no beading, and so on.[8] Perhaps it was all too French.

Britannia's designer was clearly aware of the earlier attempts at standing figures, and he pays a conscious tribute to them here. This Britannia is nevertheless a product of the 'New Sculpture', as identified by the art critic Edmund Gosse,[9] and of the aesthetic movement of the latter part of the nineteenth century. With her Symbolist, Art-Nouveau air astride a Nordic prow, facing forward – a hard-won achievement on the part of the engraver – she is now more Norse heroine than Roman matron or Greek goddess. Comparative work might be that of Alfred Stevens, whose allegorical figure of *Valour* on the Duke of Wellington's monument in St Paul's suggests subliminally a Britannia type,[10] as does F. W. Pomeroy's *Fortitude* of about 1895 for the Vestibule in Sheffield Town Hall.[11] Both were part of a new sensibility and aesthetic, which by way of the Pre-Raphaelites and such maverick sculptors as Stevens himself, rejected the inspiration of the Classical world which was seen to be stylistically derivative and technically mechanical. Pomeroy, from a younger generation, had been taught in London by the French sculptor Jules Dalou and in Paris by Antonin Mercié. The 'New Sculpture' was part of a wider change in style otherwise known in Britain as the Aesthetic Movement, and in Europe as Art Nouveau. It expressed itself in dress as well as in stone or bronze, and was satirised in

Gilbert and Sullivan's *Patience*, as the 'greenery yallery' of the Grosvenor Gallery on Bond Street. This was the gallery which under its owners Sir Coutts and Lady Lindsay did most to promote the 'New Sculpture'. It was here also that the most influential art critic of the nineteenth century, John Ruskin, first saw the work of the American artist James McNeil Whistler. He gave it such a damaging review that it prompted a libel case, after which Whistler was awarded damages of a farthing – Britannia would have been on that farthing.

Issued in 1902, De Saulles' florin was not, however, a popular or well-wearing design, and was not adopted for the lesser denominations. It was abandoned in 1911. Working with De Saulles' design 100 years later, the designer and graphic artist David Gentleman felt that the constraints of an official commission had affected the design, and in an account of his process he quoted Marion Spielman on De Saulles, describing him as 'a master of his craft and an Artist as well ... but the pressure presumably exerted on him by our official atmosphere prevented him from losing entirely the formality and neatness that British taste demands'.[12] Ironically, it may be that the image lacked tradition, but also with a breeze blowing Britannia's cloak and her stance precarious, it carried implications of change, and was just too unstable.

In the late 1890s and early 1900s Britain conducted a colonial war of expansion in South Africa, and annexed the Orange Free State and the Transvaal. There its army met with a highly-successful guerrilla resistance from the Boers. Some 500,000 British soldiers had been dispatched to the Cape, and the two phases of the war were met at home with a jingoistic enthusiasm. News of the relief of Mafeking on 17 May 1900 was celebrated by vast crowds awash with patriotic hysteria in the streets of London and elsewhere. Meanwhile in Britain, the Suffragist movement was gaining ground in its campaign for female emancipation.

As if in echo of the cheers on the streets, Britannia once again flourished on the pediments and porticos of public buildings across the nation. One spectacular example in terms of its bold statement must surely be the *Britannia* superimposed above the pediment on the main façade, looking out across the Thames, of the new National Gallery of British Art.

Above Lady Wolverhampton, Devonshire House Ball celebrating the Queen's Diamond Jubilee, 1897. Photograph. Museum of London. 60.155/55.

Below right and opposite **Designs** for the Great Seal of Edward VII, 1903, G. W. De Saulles. Pen and brown wash on board. RMM.

The gallery, designed by Sidney R. J. Smith on the site of the Millbank Penitentiary, was completed in 1897. Popularly known since its beginning as the Tate, after its benefactor, the sugar magnate Sir Henry Tate, it was officially named the Tate Gallery in 1932,[13] and became Tate Britain in 2000. The emblem survived the bomb blasts that damaged the fabric of the building in the winter of 1940 and spring of 1941. It has recently been described as 'an incongruous commission', as the sculptor Michael Lawlor, the nephew of the better-known John Lawlor, was an Irish nationalist sympathiser.[14]

At the popular end of the spectrum in the early 1900s Britannia was a constant presence at balls, fêtes, festivals, pageants and parades. Postcard Britannias were, according to Tom Phillips, the 'still' expression of 'an unembarrassed fervour for king and country'.[15] Postcards, almost always an expression of record, of the 'I was here' sort, were a popular expression of individuality, a form of aspiration and one-upmanship, as in 'Where did you go for your holidays?', to the extent that they produced a genre of their own known as 'seaside art'. They were cheap, cheerful, cost little to post, and were efficient as communication because the likelihood of their reaching their recipient before the writer returned was almost always assured. Another area in which Britannia made regular appearances was the music hall: the palaces of song and dance, stand-up comics and patterers, magicians, musicians and illusionists, all of whom made subjects for Walter Sickert and the Camden Town School of painters. Throughout the First World War, Dame Clara Butt dressed as Britannia to sing 'Land of Hope and Glory' and 'Rule Britannia', for which expression of patriotism she later received a damehood. Music halls remained hugely popular up to the advent of the Silent Screen and into the First World War, and were enjoyed by the troops on leave, when patriotic songs, the audiences joining in, raised the roof:

Are we downhearted? No!
Then let your voices ring
And altogether sing.
Are we downhearted ? No!
Not while Britannia rules the waves. Not likely![16]

The National Insurance Act of 1911 created a demand for silver and bronze coin. The bronze were sometimes struck under contract from and supervision by the Mint on Tower Hill by the independent Birmingham Mint and King's Norton Metal Co. Ltd in Birmingham.[17] These two companies continued to supply the blanks and even to strike pennies in 1912, 1918 and 1919.

G. W. De Saulles was the Mint's Engraver until his death in 1903, when the post was abolished. His design for the first and only Great Seal of Edward VII included on the obverse a standing Britannia 'playing' a three-masted sailing ship as though it were a harp. She has a globe at her feet, and is paired with Justice, while above them are positioned St Michael and St George. Thereafter, and throughout Edward VII's reign, the dies for the coinage remained De Saulles'. Acute observers will notice changes in minute detail in the penny, halfpenny and farthing where the dies have been retouched: perhaps the helmet plume becomes bifurcated, the seas more choppy, and the horizon rises and falls as time wears on.[18] These same dies were still in use for the reverse of the coin for George V, the Australian sculptor Sir Bertram Mackennal having provided the portrait for the obverse on the King's succession in 1910, and so it remained until 1936.

Above Unknown woman as *Britannia*, c. 1900. Photographic postcard. Collection of Tom Phillips.

Chapter 11

To preserve continuity in change

The handsome medal for the British Numismatic Society's commission from Frank Bowcher in 1910 is evidence of the dynamism in the design of medals of the period.[1] As the artist's brief put it, 'the obverse shall bear a device representing Britannia standing on the sea-shore and looking towards the British Dominions beyond the Seas, surrounded by the legend THE BRITISH NUMISMATIC SOCIETY'.[2] The design is still used on the Society's triennial award of the John Sanford Saltus gold medal. In the early years after the First World War, Britannia played an important role in designs for commemorative medals, some of which were of poor quality. An exception was the 'Next-of-Kin' memorial plaque, known demotically as the 'Dead Man's Penny'. Over a million of these handsome plaquettes, uniface or one-sided low-reliefs, were sent to the families of all British and Empire service personnel killed during the war, of which 600 were for women. The winner of the design competition for the plaquette, which had attracted 800 entries, was the Liverpudlian sculptor and medallist, Edward Carter Preston,[3] whose life's work would become the sculptural ornament for Giles Gilbert Scott's Liverpool Anglican Cathedral. Carter Preston's design for the plaquette may well refer to William Wyon's gentle *Una Guiding the British Lion* on the reverse of the pattern five-sovereign gold coin of 1839.[4] This, as we have seen, had been an overtly medievalising compliment to the new Queen Victoria, while the dolphins and the trident recall Wyon's Council Medal for the Great Exhibition of 1851.

The demand for good design for coins as well as official and commemorative medals led to the establishment in 1922 of the Royal Mint Advisory Committee on the Design of Coins, Medals, Seals and Decorations. This now almost 100-year-old standing committee was the brainchild of Sir Robert Johnson. Colonel Sir Robert Arthur Johnson, Deputy Master of the Royal Mint in 1922, had been commander of the 9th (Cyclist) Battalion, Hampshire Regiment throughout the First World War. His ambition was to oversee the redesign of the silver coinage, and to maintain the responsibility for commissioning design with the Mint in London. This would benefit its own workforce, restore 'aesthetic confidence', and build up 'a School of artists ... to specialise in the production of coins and medals'.[5] The Committee consisted of representatives of the arts and sciences, and included at different times the Director of Kew Gardens, for his knowledge of plants, the Keepers of Coins and Medals at the British Museum or the Heberden Coin Room in the Ashmolean Museum, Oxford, Garter King of Arms of the College of Arms, and, in a radical move, a sculptor. The first sculptor to be appointed was Francis Derwent Wood, whose Renaissance monument to the Machine Gun Corps on the north east side of Hyde Park Corner has always provoked controversy for being, variously, too naked, too

Above Sir Robert Johnson, Deputy Master of the Royal Mint, 1922-1938. National Portrait Gallery. Photograph, Bassano Ltd. NPG 151957.

Opposite 'Next-of-Kin' Memorial Plaque, 1919. Edward Carter Preston. Bronze (enlarged). RMM22,146.

conservative, and too imitatively Classical. Derwent Wood was succeeded on
the Committee by Robert Anning Bell, a follower of the Arts and Crafts
movement, and in 1932 by Charles Sargeant Jagger, whose sensationally
realist memorial to the Royal Artillery had been unveiled on the south
western edge of Hyde Park Corner in 1925. Jagger joined the Committee in
an attempt to add a dash of modernity to the group aesthetic.[6]

At the outset the dynamism in medallic design, despite Sir Robert
Johnson's initiatives, was not focused on the redesign of the silver coinage
for the United Kingdom, in spite of the need to find something new.[7]
Perhaps, after so cataclysmic a national shock as the First World War whose
effects reverberated down the century, there was within the establishment
an in-built, unvoiced resistance to change, as change was all around.
A redesigned silver coinage was eventually issued in 1927, to designs by
George Kruger Gray. His success lay, however, in energetic designs for the
coinage of the dominions and colonies, but his most popular design may
well be that for the trademark of the Suffolk brewing company Greene King.
Designs by, for example, the maverick all-round sculptor Eric Gill were
rejected.[8] A vigorous simplicity was found, however, in the new coinage
designed by Percy Metcalfe, and struck at the Mint in London for the Irish
Free State in 1928. In its intention to avoid complex emblematic meaning it
became an influential benchmark.[9]

The economic and political uncertainties of the 1920s and early 1930s,
in the General Strike of 1926, followed by the Great Crash, the Depression
and its Hunger Marches, were not conducive to the kind of positive
statement that a radical rethink of the reverse of the coinage, and the

inherent cost of it, would have entailed. In the event the Committee did not tackle a complete redesign of the coinage until a change in the head of state made it necessary in the mid 1930s. This engendered what became the Committee's greatest success: the coinage of 1936-7.

On the reverse of the multi-faceted or dodecagonal threepenny bit originally designed by Madge Kitchener, but later adapted by Percy Metcalfe, is the thrift or sea-pink, a small, hardy plant that clings to sea cliffs and is a symbol of domestic economy.[10] The nickel-brass threepenny piece was introduced in response to the sheer weight of pennies now handled daily by banks and businesses. The penny was the operative coin in most automatic machines, and the London Passenger Transport Board alone handled 600 tons of bronze coin a year.[11] The design took its cue for its simplicity and directness from the coins for the Irish Free State, a visual inheritance superficially at odds with Madge Kitchener's background as a daughter of the Raj and niece of Lord Kitchener, the Commander-in-Chief of the British forces in the First World War. She had been a 'Sladey Lady', having attended the Slade School of Art under Henry Tonks before the First World War when young women turned to art in droves, and at a time when the school was a fulcrum of creative energy. Much later Madge Kitchener would sit on the Board of British Film Censors. The reverse of the halfpenny, designed by Humphrey Paget, is a ship based on Francis Drake's three-masted *Golden Hind* in full-sail; and on the farthing, designed by Harold Wilson Parker, the wren. Designed initially for the never-to-be-crowned King Edward VIII, these designs were retained, and issued for his brother George VI in 1937, thereby losing Britannia on all but the penny.[12]

Above Threepenny bit of Edward VIII, pattern, 1937. Madge Kitchener. Nickel-brass. RMM43.

Below Penny of Edward VIII, 1937. Humphrey Paget. Bronze (enlarged). RMM50.

Britannia herself, far from responding to modernism and Art Deco, took a backward look. The new design harked back to Wyon's of 1860 with the reintroduction of a lighthouse, a little more drapery, and originally a ship, although the designer C. W. Coombes declared he had not based the figure of Britannia on anyone in particular.[13] Coombes had gone so far as to propose a Revenge class battleship, but the idea was rejected because the masts collided with the 'y' in PENNY, and was possibly considered too aggressive in the atmosphere of appeasement that prevailed right up to 1939. On the abdication of Edward VIII there was a requirement for a portrait of the new monarch, George VI. Under this innately modest man, with war looming, no changes were made to the bronze coinage as approved for Edward VIII and Britannia was again only present on the penny.[14]

There was a noticeable retreat from the avant-garde and radical art that had emerged before and during the First World War via the Slade and in the work of the Vorticists. In the 1920s the work of C. R. W. Nevinson, for example, lost its hard-edged, mechanistic manner for a softer, gentler approach to the landscape of southern England. Many artists developed, as did Stanley and Gilbert Spencer and the brothers Paul and John Nash, a romantic and idealised view of the countryside and rural life, a view that prevailed into the 1950s.

If artists, generally regarded as in advance of their times, were expressing themselves in a retrospective manner, how much more so might the establishment when looking for imagery to express those times. The caution displayed in establishment circles is well exemplified in Herbert Baker's rebuilding of the Bank of England, which began with a letter from the Deputy Governor, the Classics scholar Cecil Lubbock in 1921. This mighty project to extend the Bank's requirements for space tenfold within the existing curtilage, had to work with the constraints of history and existing architecture upon it. As Baker himself recalled, his job was 'to preserve continuity in change – a sense of permanence in progress'.[15] In aligning the old Soane colonnade on the Threadneedle Street façade with the forward thrust of Baker's inner edifice, Baker employed the young and as yet untried sculptor Charles Wheeler for a series of telemons and a high-relief figure in the pediment.[16] The new young 'Lady of the Bank' or 'Miss Threadneedle Street', was an angular and highly stylised figure intended to represent 'the stability and security of the Bank of England'.[17] Unveiled in 1929, Wheeler's sculpture, as so often, was met with derision in the popular press and elsewhere,[18] and interestingly the relief appears not to have been directly associated with Britannia. The inference is, however, obvious, and while her stylistic relation to the work of the Swedish modernist sculptor Carl Milles was remarked on,[19] this Britannia harks back not to the foundation of the Bank in the late seventeenth century, but to the wild youth at the top of the title-page of William Camden's *Britannia* of 1607.

Inside the massive building, coins, though not technically the business of the Bank, were used as the source for decoration in plaster and most successfully in mosaic. In the first floor staircase hall, it is Britannia as she appears on coins of Hadrian, 'Antonius Augustus', a halfpenny of 1672 and a penny of 1921.[20] On the ground floor, Baker, perhaps influenced by the topical and highly successful use of mosaic at the main entrance of the National Gallery, commissioned the Russian artist Boris Anrep to undertake the floors of the Threadneedle and Princes Street entrances, and those of

Above 1672 halfpenny, one of four coins depicted at the top of columns on the first floor staircase hall, Bank of England, *c.* 1930. Plaster. © The Governor and Company of the Bank of England.

Opposite **Britannia**, 1930. Sir Charles Wheeler. Portland stone. Threadneedle Street façade, The Bank of England. © The Governor and Company of the Bank of England.

the cloister-like Garden Court galleries or corridors. At the National Gallery, this whimsical artist had and continued to have fun, incorporating the portraits of well-known personalities and society figures and beauties, from Bertrand Russell, T. S. Eliot, and Edith Sitwell, to Lady Ottoline Morrell and the Hon. Mrs Brian Guinness, née Diana Mitford.[21] At the Bank of England Anrep was asked to provide a programme that gave him little room to manoeuvre, a series of Kings and Queens in mosaic roundels for the gallery floors of the Garden Court, and at the Princes Street entrance a floor design incorporating the historic coins of Hadrian, Antoninus Pius and John Roettiers.[22] The labour that this required (the artist was noted for doing much of the work himself), funding, and the outbreak of the Second World War, prevented Anrep completing the National Gallery floor until the early 1950s. He himself described the work at the Bank of England as 'a very dull, but hélas, important commission', necessitated by his own personal finances.[23] Successive Directors of the National Gallery cajoled and teased him in vain attempts to hurry it all up, expressed with a hint of facetious punning by one of them: 'I hope the sovereigns on the Bank of England foundations are finished and satisfy you and the Lubbocks of the Board'.[24] The fourth and final floor at the National Gallery was undertaken after the War, and perhaps more in the spirit of the Festival of Britain, one of the roundels, that of *Humour* in a sequence of British traits or characteristics, depicts a figure of Punch being crowned by Britannia in the person of Lady Diana Cooper.[25] It is suggested here that it may be Cooper's portrait, the quintessential English rose as Britannia, that adorns the first coloured five pound note, the 'fiver' of 1957.[26] It had been designed by Stephen Gooden, who was engaged as a designer at the Bank of England in the 1930s, and who would no doubt have been aware of Boris Anrep's mosaic personifications. The crested helmet with its shell lappets recalls the romantic *St George* of Alfred Gilbert. This retro-looking and rare attempt to give Britannia personality was not a success. The 'prettified head of Britannia (?)', note the question mark, and the overall design of the note were described in the *Architects' Journal* as 'effeminate-looking…[and] appalling'.[27]

HUMOUR

Despite the creative energies released by the end of war, opportunities for change in the coinage were not taken until the accession of Elizabeth II in 1952. The image of the new Queen on the obverse was translated from a portrait commissioned from Mary Gillick, and the reverses of silver coins were also changed. The designs of bronze coins, however, remained the same: Britannia on the reverse of the penny, and the 1937 designs of ship and wren for the reverses of the halfpenny and farthing. While the last farthing was struck in 1956, the Britannia on the penny and the ship on the halfpenny were retained right up to decimalisation in 1971.[28] This may have been an economic measure, reflecting the straitened circumstances of post-war Britain in that coins of greater value circulate in smaller numbers, but it may also have been a further example of an apparent need to express continuity and stability.

After the war Britain underwent a social and cultural revolution, and an artistic flowering that found its most public expression in 1951 in the Festival of Britain on London's South Bank. A hundred years after that other great morale-boosting exhibition, the Great Exhibition of 1851, the Festival was not so much about world trade, but more about nationhood and its future, a 'template for the reconstruction of Britain'.[29] Attracted by such temporary architectural landmarks as the Dome of Discovery and the Skylon, people came from all over the world in that long, hot summer to enjoy the wonders and the up-beat nature of the interpretation and presentation of British history and achievements.[30]

Below Penny of George VI, 1949. C. W. Coombes. Bronze (enlarged). RMM1750.

The competition to create a symbol for the Festival was won in 1948 by Abram Games, the son of a Latvian photographer and a seamstress from Russo-Poland. Games had briefly attended St Martin's School of Art to train as a graphic artist. He was eventually employed as a poster designer in the 1930s by the forward-thinking Frank Pick of London Transport, and by Jack Beddington of the petroleum company Shell, at a time when street posters were 'the art gallery of the people'.[31] During the war, as an official war artist, Games produced more than 100 posters, from recruitment to 'grow-your-own' campaigns, in which he made arresting combinations of type and text. The glamour of his Auxiliary Territorial Service (ATS) 'Blonde Bombshell' recruiting poster provoked parliamentary objections, and was withdrawn.[32] Nevertheless, he was appointed Official War Poster Designer in 1942.[33]

Games' stark image for the Festival depicted a helmeted female head making up the northern point of a compass. While conforming to Games' philosophy of 'maximum meaning through minimum means',[34] it left no one in doubt that this was Britannia. The cover of the Official Guide (price two shillings and sixpence) set the dynamic figurehead in a geometric web which suggests the scanner of aeroplane radio navigation screens, or the propellers of a turbo-prop aeroplane, carrying perhaps a subliminal message of flight, movement, and advance. The bunting on the Festival

Above Recruiting poster for the ATS, 1941. Abram Games. Photolitho print. Imperial War Museum, London. © IWM PST 2832.

Above left Design for the symbol for the Festival of Britain, 1948, on the programme for the South Bank Exhibition, 1951. Abram Games. Museum of London. 83.480/10.

symbol had been added at the request of the Festival Committee to give it
a more festive look, and was inspired, Games said, by his wife hanging out
the washing.[35] The resulting image was thus both reassuringly domestic,
and at the same time forward-looking. The emblem cropped up everywhere,
on souvenir sets of stamps, ties, tobacco tins, plastic paper knives, soap,
'and cheap tin trays'.[36] In some parts of the country, including Bedfordshire
and Suffolk where it still remains, it appeared on road signs and park
benches, but it did not appear on the coinage.[37]

In the late 1950s a very different Britannia greeted visitors to the
Coliseum on Broadway, New York: a 15-foot tall Britannia, a lion on a leash
and 20 feet of fair nylon hair flowing from under her Guardsman's helmet.
Designed by one of the leading lights of the Festival, James Gardner
for a trade fair for the Federation of British Industries, she was a foretaste
of the Swinging Sixties. Gardner had been Chief Deception Officer at the
Camouflage School at Leamington Spa where many of Britain's leading
artists found themselves working for the duration of the war. He went on to
be an influential museum and exhibition designer of the 1950s and 1960s.
As Gardner put it, Britannia was not 'that buxom dame holding a toasting
fork, but a haughty Diana the Huntress'.[38]

The symbol of Britannia was not given a new lease of life on the coinage
at this point, perhaps because she had always been a symbol of Empire. The
high-relief sculpture *Commerce and the Arts bearing Tribute to Britannia* by
W. G. Nicholl, after a design by C. R. Cockerell, in situ by 1850 on the
pediment of St George's Hall, Liverpool,[39] was removed in the 1950s, on the

pretext that it was thought to be in danger of collapse. According to the architectural historian Gavin Stamp, it is likely that it was reduced to hard core, possibly for the new motorways.[40] The architect Norman Shaw had described St George's Hall as 'one of the great edifices of the world',[41] but in 1950 it spoke of an embarrassing past that was thought no longer relevant in a city that was waking up to the effects of globalisation. The great port that for a century had carried thousands of passengers to the Americas was rapidly losing out to air transport. During the post-war years and the Cold War there were too many doubts about Britain's changing status on the world stage for Britannia to be deployed as a symbol, as India, followed by the dominions, and colonies and protectorates in Africa achieved nationhood. It is significant that in the patriotic fervour of the Falklands War of April 1982, the then Prime Minister, Margaret Thatcher, was herself all too obviously associated with Britannia by newspaper cartoonists and political commentators.[42]

Moreover, the aesthetics of the period did not lend themselves to the miniature world of coin design. The prevailing tendency in art of the immediate post-war period was Abstraction, which many artists embraced wholeheartedly. Modernist architecture largely avoided ornamental sculpture, while modern buildings for new schools and hospitals, airports and universities suited the vast canvases and murals that abstract art encouraged. Abstraction was an unsympathetic aesthetic context for coin design, heavily dependent as it is on symbolism and narrative to thrive. After

Above Cartoon of Margaret Thacher as Britannia used on the cover of *Waiving the Rules: The Constitution under Thatcherism* edited by Cosmo Graham and Tony Prosser, published by the Open University Press, 1988.
Chris Madden. Pen and ink. Ref a488.

Above British Numismatic Society
Membership Medal, 1990. John Lobban.
Bronze. RMM.

Opposite Initial designs for reverses
for the decimal coinage, 1963-4.
Christopher Ironside. Pencil on tracing
paper. British Museum, London.
BM30 &31c.

Abstraction came Pop Art with its radical tendency to subvert accepted perceptions, and inimical, like Abstraction, to the conservative need for the coinage to provide continuity and stability. With the return to figuration in the late 1970s and early 1980s, John Lobban's *Britannia* for the British Numismatic Society Membership Medal of 1990, adopted as a new look for the Society's emblem, was a neat attempt at reconciling the two opposed styles, divided between figuration and abstraction.

When the decision to decimalise the coinage seemed imminent in 1962 Christopher Ironside, who was teaching life-drawing at the Royal College of Art, submitted designs which included Britannia. In 1964 the Advisory Committee requested through the Royal Librarian, Sir Robin Mackworth-Young, a short briefing paper on the history of Britannia from Roy Strong, then Director of the National Portrait Gallery.[43] Then the Chancellor of the Exchequer and Master of the Mint, James Callaghan, made it clear that a new, public competition had to be held. In the event Christopher Ironside won, but Britannia was rumoured to be facing extinction on the coinage. Sir Bernard Braine asked in the House of Commons why this should be. As a result, Britannia, rather emaciated and shorn of context, eventually reappeared on the reverse of the new seven-sided 50 pence piece in cupro-nickel,[44] which went to trial in 1968.[45] In Ironside's many drawings one senses his difficulties, as he laboured to inject new life into a well-worn image, however one sees little variation or risk-taking as he struggled to get it right.[46] Jean Ironside was her husband's model for Britannia, and recalled posing with a ruler in lieu of a trident or a lance. As she later recounted, the domestic stress was continual as Ironside worked on these designs in official secrecy over the six years from 1962 to 1968.[47] The 50 pence piece bearing an image of Britannia was finally issued in 1969. Although superseded in terms of a variety of new designs in the last 20 years, this coin, reduced in size, remains in circulation today, embodying a 'long numismatic history' and a strong sense of tradition.[48]

If the idea of overlapping the figure is acceptable various new possibilities open up. But I would not recommend this pose in copper because it would cause confusion. C.I.

B.

Chapter 12

The utilitarian spirit of the times

....

In 1987 the Chancellor of the Exchequer, Nigel Lawson, in the face of pressure from the commercial success of the South African Krugerrand, initiated the first development for 150 years in gold coinage as legal tender, by announcing the issue of a gold bullion, one ounce coin, with Britannia on the reverse.[1] A face value of £100 made it then the highest denomination coin of the realm. The one ounce Britannia coin came also in half, quarter and tenth ounce coins which have denomination values of £50, £25 and £10. In later years new Britannia designs were struck annually, and, according to the Royal Mint's sales publicity, Britannia represented 'the changing face of Britain'. Known as 'Britannias', these coins are exempt from Capital Gains Tax, and so are purchased by bullion and other investors, a latterday version, one might be forgiven for thinking, of hoarding.

In the competition that followed the announcement by Chancellor Lawson, 52 designs by 14 designers were submitted to the Advisory Committee. The winner, Philip Nathan, declared at the time his intention of 'lessening the Neo-Classic grip and strengthening the 'British' attributes'.[2] Nathan provided a Britannia for the reverse of these essentially collectors' market coins in an eclectic variety of styles. Britannia appears on the first in 1987, a windswept figure clutching her shield and an olive branch, standing in the teeth of a gale. In design terms the composition is very much akin to that of the 1902 Edward VII florin by De Saulles, although Nathan himself disavowed this possibility as a source. In 1997 and 1999 Nathan's Britannia appears as Boudicca driving a two-horsed chariot. Her stylistic ancestors might have been Thomas Banks' roundels for the Bank of England, themselves closely modelled on the *Luna* and *Sol* reliefs on the Arch of Constantine, for Sir John Soane's Bank of England.[3] There is also a passing reference here to Thomas Thornycroft's *Boadicea* on the Embankment at Westminster Bridge. Another Nathan Britannia in retro-deco manner of 2001, in which both the woman and the lion appear to be cautiously advancing, owes something to the standing Britannia and lion on Carter Preston's bronze memorial plaquettes of the First World War, and its ultimate source is surely the image of Una and the Lion of 1839. The 2003 Britannia's helmeted head is reminiscent of French coinage depicting well-known French women, such as the film stars Brigitte Bardot and Catherine Deneuve, as Marianne, with retro-deco wave patterns suggestive of the prows of galley ships.[4]

....

Opposite One ounce proof Britannia of Elizabeth II, 1987. Philip Nathan. Gold (enlarged). RMM.

Philip Nathan has not, however, had a monopoly of the bullion coins. In 2007 Christopher Le Brun, now President of the Royal Academy, designed a romantically-embowered Britannia, her back to the Seven Sisters cliffs at Dover, her lion thoughtful as he licks a paw. It is densely composed under the diagonal of the trident, while only a leafy branch, Britannia's head, her hand holding out an olive branch, and a single-sail yacht protrude into the polished blank surface of almost half the coin. As the artist concluded 'although familiar, Britannia is a profoundly strange yet highly emotive image which still remains rich with possibility'.[5]

In 2008 the reverse for the one-ounce fine silver and gold coins was designed by John Bergdahl. This Britannia's visual roots were in the De Saulles' standing Britannia braving the seas of 1902, which in Bergdahl's interpretation appear threatening, tsunami-like, to engulf her. There is perhaps a suggestion of a King Cnut-like attitude on the part of Britannia in thus confronting the waves,[6] somehow prophetic given what happened to the world economy that year, and, close to home, the crash of Northern Rock.

The competition was won in 2010 by Suzie Zamit. Once again advances in technology allowed a change of approach, and here was the opportunity for that rare thing, a head on the reverse. The designer presented 'a new, serene portrait of the goddess',[7] thereby, according to the press release, unwittingly conferring a divinity to Britannia for the first time. Zamit explained her interpretation thus:

I wanted to portray Britannia as strong (almost Amazonian) and courageous looking, but not overly warlike; more peaceful and protective. I have given her a Corinthian-style helmet and incorporated a lion on the design: the lion being the national symbol of courage – I wanted to emphasize the strong and watchful connotations – and this also links in with Greek and Roman coinage which display many animals.[8]

In 2011 it was the turn of an erstwhile *enfant terrible* of the sculpture world, the Scottish artist David Mach.[9] Mach's *Polaris*, a life-size submarine made entirely of used car tyres displayed outside the Festival Hall on the South Bank, brought him notoriety when it was set alight by an arsonist in 1983. His design superimposed a spectre-like traditional Britannia upon a slowly waving Union Jack. In confronting the issues of Britannia in the here and now, Mach's interpretation, supported by the most sophisticated technical production methods, is, as he said at the time:

A lenticular image. The flag and Britannia appear to move reflecting a contemporary Britain; a changing Britain; a Britain which is culturally on the move but still with plenty of reasons to wave the flag.[10]

Recently, a £20 coin was issued to commemorate the centenary of the beginning of the Great War in August 1914. John Bergdahl designed the reverse of this with a standing Britannia looking out towards troop carriers in the Channel. It too is reminiscent of a De Saulles' design, that for the Queen's South Africa Medal of 1902. A further fine silver coin to the value of £50 was issued in 2015 with a design by Jody Clark. Here a teenage Britannia wearing an Athenian helmet stands before a globe, a lion resting at her feet.

In the open competition for a complete revamp of the circulating coinage issued in 2008, under the then Chancellor of the Exchequer Gordon Brown, Britannia was removed from utilitarian currency altogether. The design that was chosen was comprehensive and included all denominations in a thematic scheme akin to a puzzle.[11] In the subsequent media clamour *The Sun* newspaper sent a reporter with a live dolly-bird Britannia in red, white and blue to doorstep a member of the Advisory Committee on a Sunday morning.[12]

Britannia has since reappeared on everyday coinage. An election pledge made by David Cameron in 2010 to restore her to the circulating coinage, was honoured when the Advisory Committee proposed that she should be the subject for the design competition for the reverse of a new, bimetallic £2 coin. It was also decided that the £100 proof coin would be a reiteration of the £2 competition design. A proposed seated Britannia suckling an infant, stylistically dependent on Jules Dalou's *La Nourrice* (1873),[13] was something for which there was no precedent, and which would have made an untraditional association with *Charity*. It was dropped in the early stages

of the development of the Britannia proof series – to the relief of some of the Committee.[14] The winning designs for both coins were by Antony Dufort, and both were classic in every sense of the word. So it was that in 2015, Britannia returned to the circulating coinage on the definitive United Kingdom £2 coin.

The most interesting and inventive reworking of old ideas and old themes has been the commemorative crown for the centenary of the Entente Cordiale between Britain and France, issued by the Royal Mint in April 2004. This agreement, in which British interests in Egypt and French interests in Morocco were mutually recognised in the face of growing German expansionism, had been recorded in Frank Bowcher's *Entente Cordiale* medal at the Franco-British Exhibition of 1908.[15] David Gentleman, the designer selected for the commemorative crown from the competition in 2003, combined De Saulles' design for the silver florin of 1902 and the design by Oscar Roty for La France, the Art-Nouveau, early morning, seed-sowing *La Semeuse* so familiar on French 50 centime coins, and one and two-franc pieces. Gentleman explained his ingenious juxtaposition of:

> the national icons of Britain and France: Britannia, immortal and majestic, and La Semeuse, vigorous, alive and of the soil...the two figures merge at waist level, as if on a court card in a pack of playing cards – upright or inverted depending on which way up the coin is held. This gives equal importance to both figures, appropriate in an entente of equals.[16]

Subsequently the French Mint adopted Gentleman's design for commemorative coins of their own, the first time that they had consciously used a British design in modern times. The design of 'the sexy La Semeuse and the rather more bossy Britannia' was one of which the then Chairman of the Advisory Committee, Sir Christopher Frayling, was particularly proud.[17] It was the process involved in the design of this centenary commemorative coin that brought the iconography of Britannia on the coinage to mind, and created the subject for this book.[18]

Above Designs for reverses of one pound Bridges of Britain series; Scotland, Wales, Northern Ireland, England. Edwina Ellis. Woodcut. RMM.

Opposite £2 of Elizabeth II, 2015. Antony Dufort. Bimetallic. RMM.

Overleaf *Rule Britannia*, 1910. Frederick Spencer Gore. Oil on canvas.
© Tate, London 2016 T06521.

Conclusion

In 1906 an article in the *British Numismatic Journal* declared that 'the reason for this consistent character of modern coins is due to the utilitarian spirit of the times, and the necessity for a huge volume of money for the purposes of trade'.[19] The twentieth century might well have been called the Utilitarian Century. Low denomination coins operated much of the public utilities from public lavatories or 'conveniences' that coined the expression 'spend a penny', public transport, gas and electricity meters, to public telephones, when housed in Giles Gilbert Scott's glazed red boxes, *tempiettos* of reassurance on street corners and by woods and fields across the nation. In the middle of the century the word 'Utility', with connotations of a patriotic make-do-and-mend, usefulness and above all modernity, was adopted for clothes and furniture designed and mass produced under the aegis of the Utility Furniture Advisory Committee during and after the Second World War. This committee evolved into the influential Design Council in the post-war years, whose principles saw the emergence of mass domestic design by suppliers such as Habitat and the Swedish global company Ikea. This had become the era of the flat-pack for a new class with spending power.

In parallel has come the inflated extension of credit, introduced in the 1970s, with the dubious but seductive refrains such as 'take the waiting out of wanting', and latterly the role of companies with names like 'PayPal' which offer financial services akin to the ad hoc providers of tokens in the late seventeenth and eighteenth centuries, to manage the domestic economies of the less well off. With incipient inflation, the advent of the card economy and the use of 'plastic', and ever-developing electronic systems for payment, money changes hands in new ways. Payment by a flick of the wristwatch is here, and large volumes of coinage may become a thing of the past.

It is not altogether surprising, therefore, that Britannia has retreated to the security of the highest denominations. It is, however, in direct inverse ratio to the fiduciary principles that first sought her out and introduced her on the lowest common denominations of Charles II. A casual glance at the reverse of the coins of lower denomination and base metal over the past 300 years would suggest there has been little change in small change. However, the last two decades have seen a proliferation of designs, driven by the collectors' market, and in the case of the £1 coin once again in the race against the counterfeiters, with the result that the design of the coinage has been far from stable. This manifests itself in an increasing number of commemorative coins largely on the strangely-shaped 50 pence coin, where Britannia is still to be found in circulation.

The coin of the realm has always had a cohesive role to play, and still performs that role in, for example, the highly successful *Bridges of Britain* series designed by the Australian-born Edwina Ellis and issued from 2004 to 2007. The proliferation of commemorative coins may encourage an awareness and possibly an educative understanding of the past, and may even be discussed when children stand in dinner-line with their lunch money.

Notes

Chapter 1 Βρεταννία: a collection of islands

1 K. T. Erim 'A New Relief Showing Claudius and Britannia from Aphrodisias', *Britannia* 13 (1982), pp. 277-81.

2 In the ensuing on-line discussion, contributors did not address Beard's main issue, that of the future of Britannia; *Times Literary Supplement*, 30 January 2008, on-line; accessed 26 February 2015.

3 Erim, 1982.

4 A. M. Burnett, *Coins: Interpreting the Past*, London 1991, p. 30.

5 With the exception of L. S. Forrer, J. Toynbee, G. P. Dyer and P. P. Gaspar.

6 See, for example, L. Colley, *Britons, Forging the Nation 1707-1837*, New Haven and London 1992.

7 Exceptions, and even here the iconography has not been the thrust of the argument, are F. Saxl and R. Wittkower, *British Art and the Mediterranean*, Oxford 1948, p. 11, nos 6-11; M. Warner, *Monuments and Maidens: The Allegory of the Female Form*, London 1985; M. Pointon, 'Money and Nationalism', in G. Cubitt, *Imagining Nations*, Manchester 1998, pp. 229-54; E. Major, *Madam Britannia: Women, Church, and Nation 1712-1812*, Oxford 2012.

8 G. P. Dyer and P. P. Gaspar, *The Standing Britannia Patterns of 1788*, paper to the British Numismatic Society, January 2004. I am grateful to Graham Dyer for a copy of the text.

9 V. Hewitt, *Oxford Dictionary of National Biography*, Oxford 2004.

10 V. Heuchert, *Britannia on Coins and Banknotes*, Oxford, display and powerpoint presentation, Ashmolean Museum 2011; J. Jarrett, *Inheriting Rome: The Imperial Legacy in Coinage and Culture*, display, Barber Institute of Fine Arts, Birmingham, 2012. I am grateful to Volker Heuchert and Robert Wenley for copies of the captions.

11 F. W. Greenacre, *Marine Artists of Bristol: Nicholas Pocock and Joseph Walter*, (exhibition catalogue) City of Bristol Museum and Art Gallery 1982.

12 See the painting by or after William Clark; Glasgow Museums (1882.39)

13 Decommissioned in 1997, she is berthed as a 'Five Star Experience' at the Port of Leith, Edinburgh.

14 The proportion of pure silver was 95.8%.

15 www.antique-marks.com/antique-terms-b.html; accessed 14 March 2015.

16 P. Dobraszczyk, *Iron, Ornament and Architecture in Victorian Britain: Myth and Modernity*, Farnham, Ashgate 2014, p. 36; https://books.google.co.uk/books; accessed 25 March 2015.

17 S. Ramaswamy, *The Goddess and the Nation, Mapping Mother India*, Durham and London 2010, pp. 49-51, figs 30-1.

18 M. Myrone (ed.), *Rude Britannia: British Comic Art*, London, Tate Publishing, 2010, and the redisplay of some of the permanent collection in 2013.

19 Commissioned to record the successes of the Sydney Paralympics in 2000, it portrays Caroline Baird, Tanni Grey-Thompson, Chris Holmes, Simon Jackson, Maggie McEleny and Noel Thatcher.

20 For a full and clear account of the process see J. Craig, *The Mint. A History of the London Mint, from AD 287 to 1948*, Cambridge 1953, pp. 358-9; quoted in full in C. W. Peck, *English Copper, Tin and Bronze Coins in the British Museum 1558-1958*, London 1960, pp. 358-9; for a delightful illustrated account see D. Gentleman, *Design in Miniature*, London 1972, pp. 10-19.

21 A. Griffiths, 'The print before photography: The European print in the age of the copper plate and wooden block', University of Oxford Slade Lectures 2015; to be published by Yale University Press.

22 In 1984 the number was 67, and remains much the same today; G. P. Dyer, *The Royal Mint, An Illustrated History*, Llantrisant, The Royal Mint 1986, p. 53.

23 For a clear explanation see Peck, pp. 501-2.

24 Sybil Mignon Cooke. The work signed and inscribed: *A Julia Hommage Rodin 1907*; www.bowmansculpture.com/newsletter; accessed 28 November 2015.

25 The sculptor was Marielle Polska.

26 https://en.wikipedia.org/wiki/Marianne#Models; accessed 8 October 2015.

27 J. Barnes, 'Britannia's New Bra Size' in *Letters from London 1990-1995*, London 1995, pp. 177-91.

28 P. Attwood, 'Notorious for their Villainies', in P. Attwood and F. Powell, *Medals of Dishonour* (exhibition catalogue) British Museum 2009, pp. 15-31, fig. 7.

Chapter 2 A passion to command it

1 Tacitus, 'Agricola', in *On Britain and Germany*, H. Mattingly (trans), London 1948 (reprint 1967), p. 57.

2 There were 25 *denarii* to the *aureus*; and each *denarius* was subdivided into 4 *sestertii*, 8 *dupondii* or 16 *asses*.

3 Cassius Dio, *Historiae Romanae*, Bk 77, Section 15.

4 Armenia is personified as a youth on coins of Caesar Augustus; J. Toynbee, 'Britannia on Roman Coins of the Second Century A.D.', *Journal of Roman Studies*, 14 (1924), pp. 142-57, note 2; http://www.jstor.org; accessed 19 February 2014.

5 Barbarians of east and north were presented in long baggy trousers, *vide* the so-called *Farnese Captives*, possibly found in Trajan's Forum; Museo Nazionale, Naples; F. Haskell and N. Penny, *Taste and the Antique, the Lure of Classical Sculpture 1500-1900*, New Haven and London, 1981, catalogue 17, pp. 169-72, figs 87-8.

6 A small circular leather shield 13 inches in diameter, with an iron boss and spike, was found in 1798, when digging a drain at Caerleon, south Wales; *Archaeologia Cambrensis*, lxxx, (1924), fig. 4; referred to in J. Toynbee, 'Further Notes on Britannia Coin-Types', *Journal of Roman Studies*, 15 (1925), pp. 104-6.

7 P. Ward-Jackson, *Public Sculpture of Historic Westminster*, Liverpool 2011, pp. 340-4.

8 Probably excavated in the early sixteenth century, now Musei Capitolini, Rome; Saxl and Wittkower, p. 83, 1a; Haskell and Penny, catalogue 28, pp. 193-4, fig. 100.

9 Douglas Hamilton, 8th Duke of Hamilton, 1775; Inveraray Castle, Argyllshire; E. Peters Bowron (ed.), *Pompeo Batoni (1708-87) and his British Patrons*, (exhibition catalogue) Iveagh Bequest Kenwood 1982, note 11, and pp. 84-6, fig. 47; A. M. Clarke and E. Peters Bowron (ed.), *Pompeo Batoni. A Complete Catalogue of his Works with an Introductory Text*, Oxford 1985, catalogue 388, pl. 352.

10 George Gordon, Lord Byron, *Childe Harold's Pilgrimage*, Canto IV st 141, *Major Works*, Oxford 2000, p. 188. 'He' refers to the sculpture known as the *Dying Gladiator*; Musei Capitolini, Rome; Haskell and Penny, catalogue 44, pp. 224-5, fig. 116.

11 J. Toynbee, *The Hadrianic School: A Chapter in the History of Greek Art*, Cambridge 1934, pp. 53-65.

12 The rams' horns were emblematic of the semi-divine status he was granted by the cult of the Egyptian god Ammon.

13 A gold *stater* of Philip II carries a trident head; British Museum (1987.0649.88).

14 Scholars have debated the disappearance of the IX Legion *Hispana* and developed various inconclusive theories. For a gripping children's adventure story see R. Sutcliffe, *The Eagle of the Ninth* London 1954; for innumerable imitators, written and cinematographic, trawl the web; accessed 17 February 2015.

15 Toynbee, 1924.

16 *Exercitus Britannicus* or 'the British army'; ibid.

17 Spartianus refers to the causes in the *Vita*; quoted in Toynbee, ibid.

18 Ibid.

19 Britannia is included in what is known as the *adventus* or arrival type struck in AD 134-5. It recorded the 25 countries and cities visited by the peripatetic Emperor. In this series Britannia is presented as a standing figure holding out a *patera* or votive dish to the Emperor with an altar between them, and underscores the civil, prosperous nature of the *Pax Romana*.

20 For a discussion of the allegorical figures on the Hadrianeum, Rome, see J. Hughes,http://www.academia.edu/3105545/Personifications_and_the_Ancient_Viewer_The_Case_of_the_Hadrianeum_Nations; accessed 24 August 2015.

21 Her head is a replacement. I am grateful to Megakles Rogakos for alerting me to this image; M. Rogakos, 'Joycean Exegesis of The *Large Glass* Homeric Traces in the Postmodern Sensibility of Marcel Duchamp' unpublished PhD thesis, University of Essex, 2015.

22 For a high-relief wall tablet to John Campbell, 'of the Gibraltar Estate … Jamaica' in Bristol Cathedral see K. Eustace, 'Bread and Sermons: History in the Public Acknowledgment of Individual Lives', in F. W. Greenacre and D. Merritt, *Public Sculpture of Bristol*, Liverpool 2011, p. li, fig. 65. For other examples see N. Penny, *Church Monuments in Romantic England*, New Haven and London 1977, figs 5, 25, 47.

23 J. J. Winckelmann, *Geschichte der Kunst des Altertums* (The History of Ancient Art) 1764.

24 It has been suggested that the model was the Hadrianic *Dacia*; Toynbee 1925, pp. 104-6; http://www.jstor.org/stable/295603; accessed 19 February 2014.

25 Discussion about the significance of the globe and its comparators was magisterially summed up by Jocelyn Toynbee as 'mere conjectures, and beyond conjecture it does not seem possible to go'; ibid.

26 Ibid.

27 Toynbee, 1924, pl. xxiv.

28 Visit the British Museum/DCMS Portable Antiquities Scheme site:https://finds.org.uk/romancoins/emperors/emperor/id/23; accessed 18 August 2015.

29 I am grateful to Dr Sam Moorhead of the British Museum for drawing this to my attention; see his paper 'Carausius, Allectus and the Golden Age' given to the British Numismatic Society, 24 February 2015.

30 Tacitus, Mattingly (trans) 1967, ch. 21, p. 72.

Chapter 3 'Minerva Britanna'

1 I am grateful to John Porteous for bringing this French type to my attention, and for further discussion.

2 F. Le Blanc, *Traité Historique des Monnoyes de France*, Paris and Amsterdam, Pierre Mortier 1690 and 1692 respectively, p. 268

3 The figure of Gallia has been taken by modern scholars to be Mars, God of War, holding the little figure of Nike, the winged Victory, and sitting on a heap of arms.

4 A group of designs by Delaune survive in the Douce Bequest in the Ashmolean Museum, Oxford; J. Whiteley, 'Drawings by the Master of the "Médaillons historiques"', *Master Drawings*, XXX (1992), pp. 174-84, and J. Whiteley, *French Ornament Drawings of the Sixteenth Century*, Oxford 1996, VI, catalogue 236.

5 The documentation is recorded in J. Lafourie and P. Prieur, *Les Monnaies des Rois de France*, Paris and Basle 1956, catalogue 816, p. 61, pl. XLI.

121

6 They appear in merchants' exchange books; Hierosme Verdussen, *Carte ou Liste de chacun marq, once etc*, Antwerp 1627. Again my thanks to John Porteous for this insight.

7 R. Strong, 'Britannia: the Design. Rule Britannia', in *The Britannia Gold Bullion Coin*, Llantrisant, The Royal Mint 1987, unpaginated.

8 Quoted in full in L. B. Cormack 'Britannia Rules the Waves?: Images of Empire in Elizabethan England', *Early Modern Literary Studies*, September 1998, p. 3; http://www.shu.ac.uk/emls/04-2/cormbrit.htm, accessed 6 May 2004.

9 W. Camden, *Britannia*, London 1607; The Queen's College, Oxford (53.G.20).

10 Ibid.

11 O. D. Harris, 'William Camden, Philemon Holland and the 1610 Translation of Britannia', *Antiquaries Journal*, 95 (2015), pp. 279-303.

12 Ibid.

13 Ramaswamy, pp. 90-1, fig. 46; R. Strong, *Gloriana: The Portraits of Queen Elizabeth I*, London 1987.

14 W. L. Spiers (ed.), 'The Note-book and Account Book of Nicholas Stone', *Walpole Society*, VII (1918-9) (repr. 1969), p. 40. For an analysis of the complex iconographic detail see J. Wilson, 'The Memorial by Nicholas Stone to Sir Thomas Bodley', *Journal of the Church Monuments Society*, VIII (1993), pp. 57-62. For illustrations of Stone's design and the monument see K. Hearn, 'Art in Britain Between 1530-1620' in S. Smiles, (ed.), *West Country to World's End, the South-West in the Tudor Age*, (exhibition catalogue) Royal Albert Memorial Museum & Art Gallery 2014, pp. 64-72, pl. 11, fig. 27.

15 R. Plot, *The Natural History of Staffordshire*, Oxford 1686.

16 R. Guilding, *Owning the Past. Why the English Collected Antique Sculpture, 1640-1840*, New Haven and London 2014, p. 122, fig. 19.

17 B. Castiglione, *The Book of the Courtier*, G. Bull, (trans), Harmondsworth 1967.

18 D. Howarth, *Lord Arundel and his Circle*, New Haven and London 1985, pp. 119-21.

19 H. Peacham, *Minerva Britanna Or A Garden Of Heroical Deuises, furnished, and adorned with Emblemes and Impresa's of sundry natures*, London, W. Dight 1612 (facsimile Da Capo Press, 1971), p. 108.

20 Ibid.

21 V. Hart, *Inigo Jones, the Architect of Kings*, New Haven and London, 2011, pp. 41-55, specifically p. 46.

22 http://heritage.warwickshire.gov.uk/museum-service/collections/the-sheldon-tapestry-maps/; accessed 8 September 2015.

23 C. Avery, 'Hubert Le Seuer, the "Unworthy Praxiteles" of King Charles I', *Walpole Society*, XLVIII (1982), pp. 135-209.

24 It has, however, been suggested recently that the male infant is Britannia; Hart 2011, pp. 193-201.

25 J. Summerson, *Inigo Jones*, Harmondsworth 1966, (repr. 1983), pp. 21-3; S. Orgel and R. Strong, *Inigo Jones. The Theatre of the Stuart Court*, New York 1973.

26 Howarth, 1985, pp. 25, 31-52 *passim*, 120; K. Eustace, 'The Influence of the Antique on Sculpture in England 1610-40', unpublished MA dissertation, Courtauld Institute of Art, London 1985.

27 G. Vertue, 'Notebooks', *Walpole Society*, IV, p. 117; Orgel and Strong, I, pp. 268, 294, 346 and II, p. 461.

28 Attwood, 2009, pp. 15-31, p. 16, fig. 2.

Chapter 4 In competition with the ancient masters

1 Peck, Appendix 8h, pp. 603-4.

2 Ibid.

3 23 February 1674 *London Gazette*, quoted in Peck 1960, p. 105, and Appendix 8i, p. 604.

4 C. E. Challis, *A New History of the Royal Mint*, Cambridge 1992, p. 351.

5 Peck, p. 105. In fact, as Peck makes clear, mastery of the techniques was not achieved for more than a century.

6 1 July 1648, 'I sate for my Picture (the same wherein is a Death's head) to Mr. Walker that excellent Painter.' Originally Evelyn was depicted holding a miniature or medal of his wife. Greek and Latin inscriptions were added later; E. S. De Beer (ed.), *The Diary of John Evelyn*, Oxford 1955, II, p. 541.

7 Howarth, 1985, pp. 214-7, note 28.

8 It seems that the plaquettes may have been added later in Paris, see S. Jervis and D. Dodd, *Roman Splendour, English Arcadia, the English Taste for Pietre Dure and the Sixtus Cabinet at Stourhead*, National Trust, Philip Wilson Publishers 2014, p. 9.

9 De Beer, 1955, II, p. 343; see also p. 368.

10 Gilbert Barrell and Sir Thomas Brown; ibid., II, p. 540 and III, p. 544; Sir Robert Murray; ibid., III, p. 445; see also the list in John Evelyn, *Numismata: A Discourse of Medals Antient and Modern*, London 1697, p. 245; Bodleian Library, Oxford (XI.23). The copy examined by the writer is inscribed: Donum autoris Hans Sloane.

11 7,000 drawings which attempted a comprehensive illustrated compendium of natural and man-made objects, much of which was bought by George III, and is now in the Royal Library, Windsor Castle; De Beer, II, p. 277, and III, p. 221, note 7.

12 Evelyn 1697, p. 42.

13 De Beer, III, p. 221.

14 Ibid., pp. 106 and 385.

15 Ibid., p. 309.

16 Ibid., p. 335.

17 27 August 1663; Ibid., p. 361.

18 Ibid., p. 370.

19 A room in what had been the Inner Court of Wards, which had earlier been a royal money-making exercise, and which was abolished at the Restoration in 1660; ibid., pp. 435 and 444, and note 5.

20 Challis, p. 353. This inscription was reintroduced on the pound coin in 1983, once again as a hedge against counterfeiters.

21 Note the miniature of Sir Henry Slingsby by Nicholas Hilliard, 1595; Fitzwilliam Museum, Cambridge (3850); and monuments to Sir Henry and William Slingsby (1631 and 1634), Knaresborough Parish Church, Yorks.

22 Challis, p. 330.

23 19 February 1661; R. C. Latham and W. Matthews, *The Diary of Samuel Pepys*, London 1971.

24 Evelyn, 1697, p. 128.

25 C. Oman, *The Coinage of England*, Oxford 1931, p. 334; and Challis, p. 135.

26 Challis, pp. 365-378.

27 A silver halfpenny having long existed.

28 M. Whinney, *Sculpture in Britain 1530-1839*, Harmondsworth 1964, pp. 12-22; A. White, 'A Biographical Dictionary of London Tomb Sculptors, c.1560-c.1660', *Walpole Society*, LXI (1999), pp. 1-162.

29 The remarkable survival of which is housed in its original building now the Plantin-Moretus Museum, Antwerp.

30 De Beer, IV, p. 138 and note 2.

31 W. Petty, *Quantulumcunque, Concerning Money*, London 1682; quoted in Craig, 1953, p. 174.

32 Evelyn, 1697, p. 127, illustration LIV.

33 R. Ruding, *Annals of the Coinage of Great Britain and its Dependencies* (3rd edn), London 1840, II, p. 12 note 2; Peck, p. 111.

34 Although Charles Peck considered this a discredited theory; H. W. Morrieson, 'A review of the Coinage of Charles II', *British Numismatic Journal*, 15, (1919-20), p. 135; Peck, p. 111.

35 A. J. Marciari and C. Macleod (eds), *Painted Ladies, Women at the Court of Charles II* (exhibition catalogue), National Portrait Gallery, London 2001, catalogue 19, 20, 72.

36 12-13 and 19-20 June 1667; Latham and Matthews, 1971, VIII, pp. 262-6, 280-1.

37 F. A. Yates, *Astraea: the Imperial Theme in the Sixteenth Century*, London 1975 (reprint 1985), passim.

38 Quoted in K. Sharpe, 'Restoration and Reconstruction: Politics, Society and Culture in the England of Charles II', in Marciari and Macleod 2001, pp. 10-23, note 7.

39 From the age of 14 Louis XIV had been associated with the sun god Apollo; see *Triumph and Disaster Medals of the Sun King*, curated by Sir Mark Jones, Gallery 69a, British Museum, London 4 June - 15 November 2015.

40 The 'Wodden Walles', the ships that defended the country from the Armada, appear first in the introduction to the translation of Jan Huygen van Linschoten's *Discours of Voyages* published by John Wolfe in 1598; L. B. Cormack, 'Britannia Rules the Waves?: Images of Empire in Elizabethan England', *Early Modern Literary Studies*, September 1998, p. 6; http://www.shu.ac.uk/emls/04-2/cormbrit.htm; accessed 6 May 2004.

41 For the ideas behind monarchy and empire that continued to inform seventeenth-century thought, see Yates, *passim*.

42 Challis, pp. 338-9.

43 Oman, p. 335 and Craig 1953, p. 174

44 See Marciari and Macleod, 2001.

45 In which he made it clear that Frances Stuart had not succumbed to the blandishments of the King; G. Thorn Drury (ed.), *The Poems of Edmund Waller*, London [1905], II, p. 65.

46 'The Last Instructions to a Painter', H. M. Margoliouth (ed.), *The Poems and Letters of Andrew Marvell*, Oxford 1971, I, p.166, lines 71-4. Quoted in Marciaria and Macleod, 2001, catalogue 19.

47 Louise de Kérouaille, Duchess of Portsmouth, by Pierre Mignard, 1682. National Portrait Gallery, London (NPG 497).

48 Her funeral effigy in peeress' robe, survives among the 'ragged regiment' at Westminster Abbey. It was restored in 1934; L. E. Tanner, *Recollections of a Westminster Antiquary*, London 1969; A. D. Mackenzie, 'Britannia', *Bank Quarterly*, II, 61 (February 1934), Bank of England Archive (AB 840/3).

49 15 July 1664; Latham and Matthews IV, p. 209.

50 Marciari and Macleod, 2001, catalogue 16 and 18. In the debate as to whether Frances Stuart ever became a mistress of Charles II, it is interesting to note that her portrait appears on two occasions, one by Peter Lely and the other an enamel miniature, not in the inventory of Charles II's collection but in that of James II; Vertue, IV, pp. 93-4.

51 D. Foskett, *Samuel Cooper 1609-72*, London 1974, pp. 51, 62-79 passim.

52 Marciari and Macleod, 2001, no. 72. The date given there is 'after 1675' but with little explanation, and at the same time the Breda Medal is used as an identifying source for the sitter.

53 25 February 1667; quoted in ibid., p. 98.

54 Evelyn, 1697, p. 27.

55 W. J. W. Potter and E. J. Winstanley, *The Coinage of Henry VII*, p. 155; www.britnumsoc.org/publications/Digital%20BNJ_/.../1963_BNJ_32_11; accessed 26 August 2015. G. C. Brooke, 'The Mints of Canterbury and York in the Reigns of Edward IV and Henry VII', *British Numismatic Journal* 1931-33, pp. 73-87.

http://www.britnumsoc.org/publicati ons/Digital%20BNJ/pdfs/1963_BNJ_32 _11.pdf; accessed 26 August 2015.

56 H. W. Morrieson, 'The Silver Coins of Edward VI', *British Numismatic Journal*, 1916, pp. 137-80; http://www.britnumsoc.org/publicati ons/Digital%20BNJ/pdfs/1916_BNJ_12 _7.pdf; accessed 26 August 2015.

57 The terracotta bust of Edward VI by Michael Rysbrack (Royal Collections, Windsor Castle), and the bronze statues of Edward VI outside Guys Hospital London and in School Yard, Eton College, Windsor.

58 J. Locke, *Some Considerations on the Consequences of the Lowering of Interest and the Raising of the Value of Money*, 1691; Bodleian Library, Oxford.

59 K. Clancy, *A History of the Sovereign, Chief Coin of the World*, Llantrisant, The Royal Mint Museum 2015, p. 47.

60 Order of the Court of Directors, Bank of England, 30 July 1694; Bank of England Archive.

61 D. Byatt, *Promises to Pay: The First Three Hundred Years of Bank of England Notes*, London 1994, p. 225; confirmation: email exchange with archivists at the Bank of England, August 2015.

62 King James Bible, Psalm 19 v.10.

63 J. E. Lewis, *The English Fable: Aesop and Literary Culture, 1651-1740*, Cambridge, 1996.

64 Byatt, 1994, p. 18.

65 For which a carver was paid £7; *Britannia Quarterly*, XI, p. 9. A wooden sign in the Bank of England Collections is evidently much later, probably early nineteenth century.

66 D. M. Abramson, *Building the Bank of England: Money, Architecture, Society 1694-1942*, New Haven and London 2005, pp. 45-6, figs 53, 56.

67 H. Colvin, *A Biographical Dictionary of British Architects 1600-1840*, New Haven and London 1995, 'George Sampson', p. 841.

68 Abramson; it is not included in Roscoe, 2004; P. Ward-Jackson, *Public Sculpture of the City of London*, Liverpool 2003, pp. 26-7.

69 Quoted in Ward-Jackson, ibid. The standing figure of William III in Roman military dress is signed by Henry Cheere; Bank of England.

70 Colvin, 'Robert Taylor', p. 964.

71 Ibid.

72 This image of Britannia was the Bank's official Christmas card from 1949 to 1961; Bank of England Archive. The inner gateway from Lothbury is a reconstruction, in altered form, of Soane's Lothbury Courtyard (1798-9) with Corinthian colonnades, standing figures and relief roundels by Flaxman. It is 'now marred by a temporary glass roof'; http://www.historicengland.org.uk/en glands-places/, accessed 26 November 2015.

Chapter 5 For the use of trade

1 Peck, pp. 175-7.

2 A. Wyon, *The Great Seals of England*, London 1887, pl. XLIII, nos 153-4.

3 Peck, pp. 178-86.

4 For a full account see P. Ward-Jackson, *Public Sculpture of the City of London*, Liverpool 2003, pp. 374-81, illustration.

5 The original group was replaced by a copy by R. C. Belt and L. A. Malempré in 1884-6. The original is in a private garden at Holmhurst, Sussex; ibid.

6 T. Longstaffe-Gowan, 'Brazen proclamations: the deployment of statuary in some early London garden squares', *Sculpture Journal*, 18.1 (2009), pp. 52–66, fig. 5.

7 Peck, pp. 198-203.

8 Ibid., p. 204.

9 J. Harris, *An Essay upon Money and Coins*, 1757, quoted in Peck, p. 204.

10 F. P. Barnard, 'Forgery of English Copper Money in the Eighteenth Century', *Numismatic Circular* 1926, quoted in Peck, p. 206, note 2.

11 Peck, p. 207.

12 Ibid., pp. 206, 214-5.

13 Ibid., p. 215.

Chapter 6 Rule, Britannia!

1 Britannia was used as the promoter of indigenous genius or talent, as on the the frontispiece to William Kent's *Designs of Inigo Jones*, published in two folio volumes in 1727, under the patronage of Lord Burlington, or the dedicatory page to Thomas Johnson's rococo designs published in 1758, addressed to Lord Blakeney, Grand President of the Antigallican Association; Saxl and Wittkower, p. 53, no. 5, and B. von Preussen, '"A wild kind of imagination": eclecticism and excess in the English rococo designs of Thomas Johnson', in *Rococo Echo: Art History and Historiography from Cochin to Coppola*, M. L. Hyde and K. Scott, Oxford 2014, p. 206, fig. 9.6.

2 G. Quilley, '"All ocean is her own": the image of the sea and the identity of the maritime nation in eighteenth-century British art', in G. Cubitt (ed.), *Imagining Nations,* Manchester 1998, pp. 132-52, fig. 12.

3 The paintings have been lost and only one of them survives in an engraving; B. Allen, *Francis Hayman*, New Haven and London 1987, pp. 62-5, fig. 35; J. E. Crowley, *Imperial Landscapes: Britain's Global Visual Culture*, New Haven and London 2011, p. 6, fig. 5.

4 D. Coke and A. Borg, *Vauxhall Gardens: A History*, New Haven and London 2011.

5 For an in-depth analysis of Thomson's philosophy, politics and economics see S. Mitchell, *Visions of Britain, 1730-1830, Anglo-Scottish Writing and Representation*, Basingstoke 2013, Ch. 1, 'Thomson's Vision of Britannia', pp. 1-45, particularly p. 15.

6 Arne later presented *Britannia*, a masque at Drury Lane in 1755; Allen 1987, p. 70.

7 R. Cocke, *Public Sculpture of Norfolk and Suffolk*, Liverpool 2013, pp. 113-4.

8 F. Giacomini in C. Brooke and V. Cursi, *Hogarth Reynolds Turner, British Painting and the Rise of Modernity*, (exhibition catalogue) Fondazione Roma Museum, Rome 2014, catalogue 44, pp. 266-7.

9 He later became an MP and Groom of the Bedchamber; E. Peters Bowron (ed.), *Pompeo Batoni (1708-87) and his British Patrons*, (exhibition catalogue) Iveagh Bequest Kenwood, Greater London Council 1982, catalogue 23; Clarke and Peters Bowron, catalogue 298, col. pl. X, and pl. 273.

10 S. Jones, *Frederick, Prince of Wales and his Circle*, (exhibition catalogue) Gainsborough's House, Sudbury 1981, *passim*.

11 J. Black, 'The medal as political propaganda, a provincial example of 1739', *The Medal*, no. 10 (Winter 1986), pp. 8-10.

12 The gardens survive and are administered by the National Trust; K. Eustace, 'The Politics of the Past: Stowe and the development of the historical portrait bust', *Apollo* CXLVIII, no.437 (July 1998), pp. 31-40.

13 I. Roscoe, 'Peter Scheemakers', *Walpole Society*, LXI, (1999), pp. 163-304.

14 D. Defoe, *A Tour thro' the Whole Island of Great Britain*, III, 1742, p. 285, quoted in Roscoe, ibid., p. 274; R. Haslam, 'Concord Restored and Victory Assured', *Country Life*, CXCI no. 34 (August 21 1997), pp. 36-41.

15 J. Physick, *Designs for English Sculpture 1680-1860*, Victoria & Albert Museum, London 1969, pp. 118-21, figs 83, 84; and J. Whitlock Blundell, *Westminster Abbey, The Monuments*, London 1989, no 58, 4 illustrations.

16 Roscoe, 1999, no. 61, figs 61-2.

17 Ibid., no. 47, fig. 65.

18 Physick, pp. 130-1, figs 94-5.

19 For an account of civic-minded charity in Bristol, the country's second city in the eighteenth century, see K. Eustace, 2011, pp. xxxvii-lxv.

20 See K. Eustace, '"A Place full of rich and Industrious People": Art and patronage in Bristol in the first half of the 18th century', *British Art Journal*, VII, no.1 (Spring/Summer 2006), pp. 3-16.

21 G. Wagner, *Thomas Coram, Gent. 1668-1751*, Woodbridge 2004, *passim*.

22 Quoted in ibid., p. 140, illustration 5.

23 Ibid., p. 183, illustration 11.

24 In 1745 Michael Rysbrack proposed a marble relief entitled *Charity children engaged in navigation and husbandry* for the chimney piece of the Court Room of the Hospital. The Court Room and its contents are preserved in the Museum of what is now the Coram Foundation. The terracotta model for the relief is in the Victoria & Albert Museum, London (A.58-1953); K. Eustace, 'The key is Locke: Hogarth, Rysbrack and the Foundling Hospital', *British Art Journal*, VII no. 2, (Autumn 2006), pp. 34-49.

25 A portrait statue of Ward by Agostino Carlini, *c.* 1760, is now in the Victoria & Albert Museum, London (A.2-1991), Ward having on his death been refused a place in Westminster Abbey; M. Craske, *The Silent Rhetoric of the Body, A History of Monumental Sculpture and Commemorative Art in England 1720-1770*, New Haven and London 2007, pp. 182-3, fig. 182, and notes 101-2.

26 S. Bradley and N. Pevsner, *London 1: The City of London*, New Haven and London 1999, p. 60.

27 M. Baker, 'Sculpture for Palladian Interiors: Rysbrack's reliefs and their setting', in K. Eustace (ed.), *Michael Rysbrack Sculptor 1694-1770*, (exhibition catalogue), Bristol City Museum and Art Gallery 1984, pp. 35-41, fig. 15.

28 M. Webb, *Michael Rysbrack Sculptor*, London 1954, p. 131.

29 The British Library; http://www.bbc.co.uk/arts/your paintings/paintings/the-east-offering-its-riches-to-britannia-191140; accessed 4 December 2015.

30 Bradley and Pevsner, 1999, p. 93.

31 Bacon's second wife Martha was a sister of the architect Henry Holland.

32 Ward-Jackson, 2003, p. xix.

33 M. Baker and D. Bindman, *Roubiliac and the Eighteenth-Century Monument, Sculpture as Theatre*, New Haven and London 1995, plates I-XV; and Craske 2007, pp. 89-106.

34 Ward-Jackson, 2003, pp. 163-6.

35 Ibid., pp. 166-70, illustrated. The memorial suffered from serious bomb damage in the Second World War, and was unsatisfactorily restored.

36 Quoted in full, ibid., pp. 170-3.

37 Roscoe, *et al* 2009.

38 Quoted from the sculptor's proposal in Ward-Jackson 2003, pp. 173-7. This conceit is used in 1848 on a monument to the Third Sutlej Campaign by George Nelson in Canterbury Cathedral; K. Eustace, 'Post-Reformation Monuments', in P. Collinson, N. Ramsay, and M. Sparks (eds), *A History of Canterbury Cathedral*, Oxford 1995 (2nd ed. 2004), p. 542, pl. 156.

39 Haskell and Penny, pp. 148-51 and 266-7.

40 Quoted in Ward-Jackson, 2003, p. 175.

41 Ibid., pp. 177-81.

42 B. Read, *Victorian Sculpture*, New Haven and London 1982, p. 91.

43 Ibid., *passim*.

Chapter 7 The protecting power or genius of the country

1 Both Wedgwood and Boulton's monuments, in Stoke-on-Trent (1803) and Handsworth Birmingham (1810-3), were commissioned from John Flaxman; Penny, 1977, p. 177, fig. 130.

2 A. Cox-Johnson, *John Bacon RA 1740-99*, St Marylebone Society Publication no. 4, 1961.

3 S. Tungate, 'Matthew Boulton's Mints: Copper to Customer', in S. Mason (ed.), *Matthew Boulton. Selling what all the world desires*, (exhibition catalogue) Birmingham City Art Gallery, New Haven and London 2009, pp. 81-8.

4 D. Bindman (ed.), *John Flaxman 1755-1826, Master of the Purist Line*, (exhibition catalogue) Sir John Soane's Museum and University College London 2003.

5 J. Flaxman, *Lectures on Sculpture*, London 1838; Royal Academy Collections (07/4623).

6 G. Pollard, 'Flaxman and designs for medals and coins', in D. Bindman (ed.), *John Flaxman RA*, (exhibition catalogue) London, Royal Academy 1979, pp. 135-40.

7 For a full and excellent account of what that entailed see Tungate in Mason 2009.

8 D. Symonds, '"Bringing to Perfection the Art of Coining": what did they make at the Soho Mint?' in ibid., pp. 89-98, fig. 69, p. 214, nos 298-306.

9 Quoted in ibid.

10 Ibid., p. 90, fig. 68.

11 J. Porteous, *Coins in History*, London 1969, p. 229, fig. 270.

12 Ibid., p. 98, note 47.

13 G. P. Dyer and P. P. Gaspar, *The Standing Britannia Patterns of 1788*, paper to the British Numismatic Society, January 2004; Peck, p. 234.

14 Peck, p. 317.

15 Ibid.

16 Dyer and Gaspar, 2004.

17 I am most grateful to Graham Dyer for this reference; 14, 28 March, 1 June 1797, National Archives Privy Council Committee on Coin (BT6/126).

18 J. Uglow, 'Matthew Boulton and the Lunar Society', in S. Mason (ed.) 2009, pp. 7-13; J. Uglow, *The Lunar Men The Friends who made the Future*, London 2002 (paperback ed. 2003).

19 Bindman, 1979, catalogue 52 a-e.

20 Quoted in ibid.

21 Physick, pp. 146-7, figs 110-11.

22 K. Eustace, 'Robert Adam, Charles-Louis Clérisseau, Michael Rysbrack and the Hopetoun chimneypiece', *Burlington Magazine*, CXXXIX, November 1997, pp. 743-52.

23 Haskell and Penny, catalogue 63, fig. 140.

24 G. Seidmann, 'Nathaniel Marchant, Gem-engraver, 1739-1816', *Walpole Society*, LIII (1990), pp. 1-107.

25 L. Schorn, Kunst-Blatt (Weimar, 1827), quoted in Bindman 1979, p. 30.

26 D. Irwin, *John Flaxman, 1755-1826, Sculptor, Illustrator, Designer*, London 1979, p. 160.

27 A third life-size cast of *Britannia* is in the Sir John Soane's Museum, Lincolns Inn Fields, London; Physick, pp. 165-9, figs 129-30.

28 J. Flaxman, *Letter to the Committee for Raising the Naval Pillar under the Patronage of his Royal Highness the Duke of Clarence 1799*; National

Maritime Museum Library. The competition for a monument in Trafalgar Square was eventually won in 1839 when the military engineer Henry Railton proposed a column and E. H. Baily, Flaxman's former pupil and successor, proposed a colossal figure, no longer of Britannia, but of the naval hero Admiral Lord Nelson himself. See also Ward-Jackson, 2011, pp. 274-88.

Chapter 8 Una guides the British Lion

1 Ward-Jackson, 2011, p. 164.

2 Victoria & Albert Museum (A.14-1939); ibid., p. 165, illustrated.

3 Ibid., pp. 293-5.

4 Chantrey's equestrian George IV remained in his studio until after the sculptor's death when it was set up on a plinth in Trafalgar Square in 1843, and remains there; ibid., p. 295.

5 S. Bradley and N. Pevsner, *London 6: Westminster*, New Haven and London 2003, p. 446.

6 R. Sainthill, *An Olla Podrida or Scraps, Numismatic, Antiquarian and Literary*, II, London 1853, p. 7.

7 The unofficial title 'Principal Engraver and Chief Medallist' was applied by his biographer Michael Marsh in *Benedetto Pistrucci Principal Engraver and Chief Medallist of the Royal Mint*, Hardwick 1996.

8 Clancy, 2015, pp. 58-63, illustrated.

9 K. Eustace (ed.), (exhibition catalogue) *Canova Ideal Heads*, Ashmolean Museum, Oxford 1997, catalogue 13.

10 The Bank of England had had an earlier token for 5 shillings with Britannia on it. St George had appeared on the 'George Nobles' of Henry VIII in 1526, and on the Petition crown of the 1660s; Clancy 2015, pp. 58-9.

11 Peck, p. 390. The 1821 design was replaced in 1825.

12 Ibid., p. 406.

13 The design was extended to the silver groat in 1836; ibid. Peck makes the point that the correct rendering of the Union Flag was never fully achieved.

14 Ibid., fig. 34; and Eustace 1997, *passim*.

15 P. Attwood, *Hard at Work, the Diary of Leonard Wyon 1853-1867*, London 2014, p. 17; Gentleman, 1972, p. 74.

16 Attwood, 2014, pp. 9-10.

17 See S. Piggott, *William Stukeley An Eighteenth-Century Antiquarian*, Hungary 1950 (rev. 1985), *passim*; S. Smiles, *The Image of Antiquity, Ancient Britain and the Romantic Imagination*, New Haven and London 1994; K. Eustace, 'The Politics of the Past: Stowe and the development of the historical portrait bust', *Apollo*, CXLVIII, no. 437 (July 1998), pp. 31-40; O. Cox, 'The Cult of Alfred', in S. Parissien, *Celebrating Britain, Canaletto, Hogarth and Patriotism*, London 2015, pp. 97-118.

18 M. Jones, *The Art of the Medal*, London 1979, no. 280, illustrated; Clancy 2015, pp. 69-70, illustrated.

19 M. Girouard, *The Return to Camelot: Chivalry and the English Gentleman*, London and New Haven 1981, pp. 88-110.

20 Peck suggests that this pattern was obtained from the five-pound punch via the reducing machine; Peck, p. 458, pl. 41, no. 1993.

21 Attwood, 2014, p. 21, fig. 21.

22 19 and 21-24 November 1860; ibid., pp. 228-9.

23 Peck, p. 419, note 5.

24 Ibid., pp. 416-9.

25 7 December 1860; Attwood 2014, p. 229.

26 Conversation with Mark Jones, March 2015.

27 16 December 1860; Attwood 2014, p. 230.

28 6 January 1861; ibid., p. 246.

29 Peck, plates 33-4.

30 Ibid., pp. 446-7.

31 Ibid.

Chapter 9 Looking at an image of Victoria

1 P. J. Marshall (ed.), *The Eighteenth Century*, Oxford 2001, *passim*.

2 Ibid., specifically pp. 112, 114.

3 Attwood, 2014, appendices pp. 327-9.

4 19 December, 16, 26 January 1860; ibid., pp. 230-2.

5 See illustrations in Attwood; ibid., pp. 326-7.

6 16, 23 February, 7 March; ibid., p. 233.

7 Ramaswamy, p. 11, figs 5, 5a, and p. 79.

8 Two designs survive in the Victoria & Albert Museum. Flaxman received an advance 'on account' in 1811 and the final payment in 1816; Physick, pp. 174-5, figs 134-5.

9 Later manifestations include Wilfred Thesiger's experience and presentation of the nomads of the Arabian Peninsula and Eastern Africa.

10 The die broke in hardening, and there was no time to re-engrave it; Sainthill 1844, I, p. 28, plate 1.

11 De Nobili, known as the white Brahmin, provided a synthesis of the Dharma of Hinduism with Christianity; V. Cronin, *A Pearl to India: The Life of Roberto de Nobili*, London 1959.

12 Sainthill, 1853, II, pp. 89-102.

13 'Suggestions that Medals for the Indian Army should be Indian in Ideas, and in the Language used for Inscriptions'; ibid., pp. 103-6.

14 Ibid., p. 103, and footnote.

15 Ibid, p. 106.

16 Quoted in Ramaswamy, p. 91; R. Strong, *Gloriana: The Portraits of Queen Elizabeth I*, London 1987, p. 99.

17 Ramaswamy, p. 82.

18 Attwood, 2014, p. 20, fig. 21.

19 I am grateful to Shailendra Bhandare for discussing this and other images with me; Ramaswamy, p. 80, fig. 41.

20 J. Gifford, *et al.*, *Edinburgh*, New Haven and London, p. 289.

21 Steell had proceeded to a full-scale clay model when on the accession of the new Queen the Board of Manufacturers changed their mind; see R. Lieuallan, 'A Sculptor for Scotland: The Life and Work of Sir John Steell RSA (1804-1891)', PhD Diss, 2 vols, Edinburgh University 2002, I, pp. 122-36, and II, catalogue 29, illustrated; www.era.lib.ed.ac.uk (pdf 174. 9Mb and 110. 7Mb); accessed 8 March 2016.

22 E. Martin, 'Framing Victoria: royal portraiture and architectural sculpture in Victorian Britain', *Sculpture Journal*, 23.2 (2014), pp. 197-207, fig. 1.

23 Read, pp. 97-103, 155-64.

24 An oil sketch for this was sold from the Forbes Collection, Lyon and Turnbull, 1 November 2011, Lot 147.

25 L. Hawksley, *The Mystery of Princess Louise, Queen Victoria's rebellious daughter*, London 2014, pp. 225-6, 280-1, illustrated.

26 Another 77 were raised after her death; Martin, 2014.

27 S. Beattie, *The New Sculpture*, New Haven and London 1983, p. 230.

28 Ward-Jackson, 2011, pp. 125-31.

29 Bradley and Pevsner, 2003, p. 654.

Chapter 10 An unembarrassed fervour for king and country

1 Quoted in C. P. Barclay, 'G. W. De Saulles, Engraver to the Mint', *The Medal*, no. 20 (Spring 1992), pp. 56-68.

2 18 June 1896, *Punch*; ibid.

3 Ibid.

4 Sir Charles Fremantle, Deputy Master of the Mint, letter to the *Daily Telegraph*, 31 January 1893; quoted in ibid.

5 K. Clancy, 'The British Trade Dollar', *Oriental Numismatic Newsletter*, no. 169 (Autumn 2001), pp. 25-9.

6 Ibid.

7 Drawings were thought to have survived with the family, but the present writer has been unable to establish this with the St Aldwyns Estate Office.

8 'Varia: The New Florin', *Daily Graphic*; Spink & Son, *Numismatic Circular* (July 1904).

9 The title of an article by Edmund Gosse published in the *Art Journal*, March 1893; see S. Beattie, *The New Sculpture*, New Haven and London 1983, p. 3.

10 *Valour and Cowardice*, full-size plaster model; Victoria & Albert Museum (321:B-1878); D. Bielby with M. Trusted, *British Sculpture 1470 to 2000. A concise catalogue of the collection at the Victoria & Albert Museum*, London 2002, catalogue 581; N. Penny, *Catalogue of European Sculpture in the Ashmolean. 1540 to the Present Day*, Oxford 1992, III, catalogue 571.

11 Beattie, pp. 4, 61-4; D. White and E. Norman, *Public Sculpture of Sheffield and South Yorkshire*, Liverpool 2015.

12 M. H. Spielman, *British Sculpture and Sculptors of Today*, London 1901; quoted in D. Gentleman, 'Britannia and La Semeuse', *Fleur de Coin Review*, Issue 23, December 2004, pp. 4-7.

13 F. Spalding, *The Tate, a History*, Over Wallop 1998, p. 65.

14 P. Murphy, *Nineteenth Century Irish Sculpture, native genius reaffirmed*, New Haven and London 2010, p. 181; T. Snoddy, *Dictionary of Irish Artists, 20th Century*, Dublin 2002 (2nd ed.).

15 T. Phillips, *We Are the People: Postcards from the Collection of Tom Phillips*, (exhibition catalogue) National Portrait Gallery, London 2004, p. 117.

16 Revamped for Joan Littlewood's *Oh, What a lovely War!* in 1963; subsequently a film directed by Richard Attenborough in 1969, starring Vanesa Redgrave, Maggie Smith, Laurence Olivier, Ralph Richardson and John Guilgud.

17 In 1912, 1918, and 1919; I am grateful to Graham Dyer for this information.

18 Peck, pp. 497-500.

Chapter 11 To preserve continuity in change

1 Fitzwilliam Museum, Cambridge (CM.832-2012).

2 http://www.britnumsoc.org/publications/Digital%20BNJ/pdfs/1910_BNJ_7_13.pdf; accessed 23 March 2015.

3 'Bronze Memorial Plaques - Notes on origins, history & identification', *Commonwealth War Graves Commission*; on-line: en.wikipedia.org/wiki/Memorial_Plaque_(medallion); accessed 21 March 2015.

4 Jones 1979, no. 280, illustrated.

5 Quoted in C. Frayling, 'Continuity through change: the Royal Mint Advisory Committee', in K. Clancy (ed.), *Designing Change: The Art of Coin Design*, Llantrisant 2008, pp. 39-65. Kevin Clancy informs me that requests for designs were always out-sourced in this period.

6 In 1998 when the present author was appointed a member of the Committee, the President, HRH Prince Philip, responded to her first intervention with gentle irony: 'Innovation is not a word we use on this Committee'.

7 Conversation between the author and Kevin Clancy.

8 The Royal Mint Museum; illustrated in S. Raw, 'The visual language of coins', in Clancy 2008, pp. 86-7.

9 This was the intention of W. B. Yeats, Chairman of the design committee; avoidance itself imbued the designs with meaning and significance; Brian Cleeve (ed), *W. B. Yeats and the Designs of Ireland's Coinage*, Dublin and New York 1972; T. Mohr, 'The British Empire and the Coinage of the Irish Free State', www.academia.edu/1905525; accessed 3 November 2015; Frayling in Clancy 2008, pp. 48-51, illustrated.

10 The design was later modified by Percy Metcalfe, to which Kitchener took exception, feeling her intentions had been traduced; information from Graham Dyer.

11 Peck, p. 513.

12 G. P. Dyer, *The Proposed Coinage of King Edward VIII*, HMSO 1973; Peck, p. 510.

13 The Royal Mint Museum archive.

14 Peck, p. 514.

15 H. Baker, *Architecture and Personalities*, London 1944, Ch. 8, 'Practice in London', pp. 122-31, illustrated p. 123.

16 H. Baker, *The Decoration in the New Bank of England and its Significance*, London 1939; S. Crellin, *The Sculpture of Charles Wheeler*, London 2013, pp. 36-48, figs 25, 29; Ward-Jackson 2003, p. 16.

17 Baker, 1939.

18 Crellin, pp. 40-1.

19 Ibid.

20 Baker, 1939.

21 L. Oliver, *Boris Anrep, The National Gallery Mosaics*, London 2004.

22 Baker, 1939, p. 10. The centre of the floor with its Wheeler-inspired Britannia is currently hidden by a large architectural model of the Bank.

23 National Gallery Archive (7.27.1/2 Anrep Boris 1927-1933, 1945-1952).

24 Sir Augustus Daniel to Boris Anrep, 7 October 1932; ibid.

25 As Lady Diana Manners, daughter of the Duke of Rutland, she had starred as a statue in Max Reinhart's *The Miracle on Broadway* in 1923. She married the successful politician and diplomat, Duff Cooper, Ambassador to France in the post-war years, ennobled Viscount Norwich; D. Cooper, *Autobiography*, 3 vols, London 1958-60.

26 J. Keyworth, *Security by Design. A closer look at Bank of England Notes*, London, Bank of England Museum, 2007, p. 7.

27 Quoted in D. Byatt, *Promises to Pay: The First Three Hundred Years of Bank of England Notes*, London, Spink 1994, p. 166, illustrated.

28 Peck, pp. 522-7.

29 P. Rennie, *Festival of Britain Design 1951*, Woodbridge 2007 (reprint 2008), p. 19.

30 M. Banham and B. Hillier (eds), *A Tonic to the Nation. The Festival of Britain*, London 1976, *passim*.

31 N. Games and B. Webb, *Abram Games Design*, Woodbridge 2013, p. 11.

32 ATS is an abbreviation of Auxiliary Territorial Services, formed in 1938. Initially it was a women's voluntary service, but in 1949 it was merged into the Women's Royal Army Corps; ibid., pp. 14-5, illustrated.

33 C. McDermott, *Masterpieces of Modern Design*, Hong Kong 2013, p. 292.

34 Rennie, p. 24.

35 C. Moriarty (ed.), *Abram Games: Maximum Meaning Minimum Means* (exhibition catalogue) Design Museum, London 2003.

36 J. Masefield, *Cargoes*, first published 1902, 1944.

37 W. Feaver, 'Festival Star', in Banham and Hillier, p. 40.

38 J. Gardner, *The Artful Designer, ideas off the drawing board*, London 1993, pp. 253-4, illustrated.

39 Read, p. 220.

40 G. Stamp, 'Architectural Sculpture in Liverpool', in P. Curtis, *Patronage & Practice Sculpture on Merseyside*, Liverpool 1989, pp. 8-12, fig. 2.

41 Quoted in ibid.

42 Warner, pp. 38-45.

43 R. Strong, 'A Note on Britannia'; The Royal Mint Museum archive files. Graham Dyer remembers that Ironside's difficulties may have occasioned the request from the Advisory Committee for help, well before Bernard Braine's intervention. Advisory Committee Minutes of 151st meeting 29 April 1964. Strong, 1987, unpaginated.

44 The technical term for the shape of a 50 pence is an equilateral curve heptagon.

45 C. Eagleton, 'Christopher Ironside and the designs for the decimal coinage', and K. Clancy, 'Receiving change: reaction to the new designs', in Clancy 2008, pp. 23 -37, and 97, illustrated.

46 The British Museum holds the Ironside design archive.

47 J. Ironside, 'Don't Run up a Flag', *Fleur de Coin Review*, (1997), pp. 7-9.

48 Quoting the then Deputy Master of the Mint, Sir Jack James; Frayling in Clancy 2008, pp. 39-65.

Chapter 12 The utilitarian spirit of the times

1 Four coins were issued as part of the series: £100 – one ounce; £50 – half ounce; £25 – quarter ounce; and £10 – tenth of an ounce.

2 P. Nathan, 'A British Britannia', in *The Britannia Gold Bullion Coin*, Llantrisant 1987, unpaginated.

3 J. Bryant, *Thomas Banks 1735-1805 Britain's First Modern Sculptor*, (exhibition catalogue) Sir John Soane's Museum, London 2005, catalogue 40-50.

4 Nathan states that he deliberately avoided De Saulles' standing Britannia, and all other earlier representations, while admitting that no artist works in a vacuum; Nathan, 1987.

5 K. Clancy (ed.), *The Royal Mint Collector Coins, the story behind the 2007 collection*, Huddersfield 2006, p. 60.

6 Clancy, 2008, p. 72.

7 Press release, The Royal Mint; http://www.royalmint.com/aboutus/news/the-enduring-icon-of-britain; accessed 22 January 2015.

8 http://talismancoins.com; accessed 30 October 2015.

9 Mach's *Polaris*, a life-size submarine made entirely of car tyres was set alight, when displayed in 1983, by an arsonist on the South Bank, London.

10 http://www.royalmint.com/discover/britannia/david-mach-ra; accessed 2 October 2015.

11 Clancy, 2008, pp. 67-79.

12 John Porteous in conversation with the author; and the Royal Mint Museum archive (cuttings).

13 Victoria & Albert Museum, London (A.8-1993); Fitzwilliam Museum, Cambridge (M.3-1927).

14 Advisory Committee Minutes; the Royal Mint Museum archive.

15 Victoria & Albert Museum, London (A.78-1978).

16 Artist's design presentation to the Royal Mint Advisory Committee, 2003; for an account of the design inspiration and process see Gentleman 2004, pp. 4-7.

17 C. Frayling, 'Continuity through change: the Royal Mint Advisory Committee', in Clancy 2008, pp. 39-65.

18 The author presented a paper at the British Numismatic Society summer meeting, Canterbury 2005, later published; Eustace 2006.

19 S. H. Hamer, Notes on the private tokens, their issuers and die-strikers, *British Numismatic Journal*, 1-3, pp. 271-4, 369-96.

Britannia on Roman coins and medallions

The following catalogue provides a selection of the representations of Britannia on Roman coins and medallions. Only the relevant part of the reverse inscription is normally given.

Opposite Weeping Province, AD 117, keystone used as a pedestal for a figure of *Roma*. Musei Capitolini, Rome.

Ruler	Hadrian
Denomination	**As**
Date	*c.* AD 119
Inscription	BRITANNIA (in exergue)
Material	Copper
Collection	British Museum 1935,0404.57

Ruler	Hadrian
Denomination	**Sestertius**
Date	*c.* AD 135
Inscription	EXERC BRITANNICUS
Material	Brass
Collection	British Museum BMC 1672

Ruler	Hadrian
Denomination	**Sestertius**
Date	AD 134-5
Inscription	BRITANNIA
Material	Brass
Collection	British Museum 1723

Ruler	Antoninus Pius
Denomination	**Sestertius**
Date	*c.* AD 143
Inscription	BRITANNIA
Material	Brass
Collection	British Museum 1637

Ruler	Antoninus Pius
Denomination	**Sestertius**
Date	c. AD 143
Inscription	IMPERATOR II; BRITAN (in exergue)
Material	Brass
Collection	British Museum BMC 1640

Ruler	Antoninus Pius
Denomination	**As**
Date	AD 154
Inscription	BRITANNIA. COS IIII
Material	Copper alloy
Collection	British Museum 1959,0305.35

Ruler	Commodus
Denomination	**Sestertius**
Date	AD 184-5
Inscription	BRIT (in exergue)
Material	Brass
Collection	British Museum 1971,1001.2

Ruler	Carausius
Denomination	**Denarius**
Date	c. AD 286-93
Inscription	EXPECTATE VENI
Material	Silver
Collection	British Museum 1935,0404.57

Ruler   Commodus
Date   AD 180-92
Material   Copper alloy
Inscription BRITTANIA (sic) P M TR P X IMP VII COS IIII P P
Collection British Museum BMC Medallions Commodus 12

Ruler   Carausius
Date   c. AD 287
Material   Copper alloy
Inscription Obverse: IMP C [M]AV CARAVSIVS P F AVG GER
             Reverse: VICTOR CARAVSIVS AVG [GER]M MAX
Collection British Museum 1972,0717.1

Britannia on British circulating coins 1672-2015

The following catalogue provides a selection of the representations of Britannia on British circulating coins since 1672.

Monarch	Charles II
Date	1672
Denomination	Halfpenny
Material	Copper
Obverse	J. Roettiers
Reverse	J. Roettiers
	RMM719

Monarch	James II
Date	1685
Denomination	Halfpenny
Material	Tin with copper plug
Obverse	J. Roettiers
Reverse	J. Roettiers
	RMM775

Monarchs	William & Mary
Date	1694
Denomination	Halfpenny
Material	Copper
Obverse	Uncertain
Reverse	J. Roettiers
	RMM803

Monarch	William III
Date	1699
Denomination	Halfpenny
Material	Copper
Obverse	J. Roettiers
Reverse	J. Roettiers

RMM930

Monarch	Queen Anne
Date	1714
Denomination	Farthing
Material	Copper
Obverse	J. Croker
Reverse	J. Croker

RMM459

Monarch	George I
Date	1717
Denomination	Halfpenny
Material	Copper
Obverse	J. Croker
Reverse	J. Croker

RMM349

Monarch	George II
Date	1731
Denomination	Halfpenny
Material	Copper
Obverse	J. Croker
Reverse	J. Croker

RMM549

Monarch	George III
Date	1797
Denomination	Cartwheel penny
Material	Copper
Obverse	C. H. Küchler
Reverse	C. H. Küchler
	RMM1086

Monarch	George IV
Date	1823
Denomination	Farthing
Material	Copper
Obverse	B. Pistrucci
Reverse	W. Wyon
	RMM1358

Monarch	George IV
Date	1826
Denomination	Penny
Material	Copper
Obverse	W. Wyon after Chantrey
Reverse	W. Wyon
	RMM1343

Monarch	William IV
Date	1836
Denomination	Groat
Material	Silver
Obverse	W. Wyon after Chantrey
Reverse	W. Wyon
	RMM129

Monarch	Victoria
Date	1860
Denomination	Penny
Material	Bronze
Obverse	L. C. Wyon
Reverse	L. C. Wyon

RMM4228

Monarch	Victoria
Date	1895
Denomination	Penny
Material	Bronze
Obverse	T. Brock
Reverse	G. W. De Saulles

RMM4260

Monarch	Edward VII
Date	1902
Denomination	Florin
Material	Silver
Obverse	G. W. De Saulles
Reverse	G. W. De Saulles

RMM223

Monarch	George V
Date	1911
Denomination	Penny
Material	Bronze
Obverse	B. Mackennal
Reverse	G. W. De Saulles

RMM2188

Monarch	George VI
Date	1938
Denomination	Penny
Material	Bronze
Obverse	T. H. Paget
Reverse	C. W. Coombes
	RMM1742

Monarch	Elizabeth II
Date	1953
Denomination	Penny
Material	Bronze
Obverse	M. Gillick
Reverse	C. W. Coombes
	RMM2828

Monarch	Elizabeth II
Date	1969
Denomination	Fifty pence
Material	Cupro-nickel
Obverse	A. Machin
Reverse	C. Ironside
	RMM

Monarch	Elizabeth II
Date	2015
Denomination	£2
Material	Inner: Cupro-nickel
	Outer: Nickel-brass
Obverse	J. Clark
Reverse	A. Dufort
	RMM

Britannia on British bullion coins 1987-2015

The following catalogue provides a selection of the representations of Britannia on British bullion coins since 1987. Each of these designs has been used on a range of denominations and, from 1997, produced in silver as well as gold.

Monarch	Elizabeth II
Date	1987
Denomination	£100
Material	Gold
Obverse	R. Maklouf
Reverse	P. Nathan
	RMM.

Monarch	Elizabeth II
Date	1997
Denomination	£100
Material	Gold
Obverse	R. Maklouf
Reverse	P. Nathan
	RMM

Monarch	Elizabeth II
Date	2001
Denomination	£100
Material	Gold
Obverse	I. Rank-Broadley
Reverse	P. Nathan
	RMM

Monarch	Elizabeth II
Date	2003
Denomination	£100
Material	Gold
Obverse	I. Rank-Broadley
Reverse	P. Nathan
	RMM

Monarch	Elizabeth II
Date	2005
Denomination	£100
Material	Gold
Obverse	I. Rank-Broadley
Reverse	P. Nathan

RMM

Monarch	Elizabeth II
Date	2007
Denomination	£100
Material	Gold
Obverse	I. Rank-Broadley
Reverse	C. Le Brun

RMM

Monarch	Elizabeth II
Date	2008
Denomination	£100
Material	Gold
Obverse	I. Rank-Broadley
Reverse	J. Bergdahl

RMM

Monarch	Elizabeth II
Date	2010
Denomination	£100
Material	Gold
Obverse	I. Rank-Broadley
Reverse	S. Zamit

RMM

Monarch	Elizabeth II
Date	2011
Denomination	£100
Material	Gold
Obverse	I. Rank-Broadley
Reverse	D. Mach
	RMM

Monarch	Elizabeth II
Date	2013
Denomination	£100
Material	Gold
Obverse	I. Rank-Broadley
Reverse	R. Hunt
	RMM

Monarch	Elizabeth II
Date	2014
Denomination	£100
Material	Gold
Obverse	I. Rank-Broadley
Reverse	J. Clark
	RMM

Monarch	Elizabeth II
Date	2015
Denomination	£100
Material	Gold
Obverse	J. Clark
Reverse	A. Dufort
	RMM

Bibliography

Anon., 'Varia: The New Florin' (extract from the *Daily Graphic*), *Numismatic Circular*, July 1904.

Aristotle, *The Ethics*, J. A. K. Thomson, (trans), Harmondswoth, Penguin Classics 1953 (reprint 1966).

Abramson, D. M., *Building the Bank of England: Money Architecture Society 1694-1942*, New Haven and London, Yale University Press 2005.

Allen, B., *Francis Hayman*, New Haven and London, Yale University Press 1987.

Allen, B., 'From Plassey to Seringapatam: India and British History Painting c.1760-c.1800', in C. A. Bayly, (ed.), *The Raj India and the British 1600-1947* (exhibition catalogue), London, National Portrait Gallery 1990.

Attwood, P., and Powell, F., *Medals of Dishonour* (exhibition catalogue), London, British Museum Press 2009.

Attwood, P., *Hard at Work, the Diary of Leonard Wyon 1853-1867*, London, British Numismatic Society, BNS Special Publication No.9, 2014.

Avery, C., 'Hubert Le Seuer, the "Unworthy Praxiteles" of King Charles I', *Walpole Society*, vol. XLVIII, 1982, pp. 135-209 republished in C. Avery, *Studies in European Sculpture, London*, Christie's 1988.

Baker, H., with illustrations by Charles Wheeler, *The Decoration in the New Bank of England and its Significance*, London, Governor and Company of the Bank of England 1939.

Baker, H., *Architecture and Personalities*, London, Country Life Ltd. 1944.

Baker, M., see Eustace 1982.

Baker, M., and Bindman, D., *Roubiliac and the Eighteenth-Century Monument, Sculpture as Theatre*, New Haven and London, Yale University Press 1995.

Banham, M., and Hillier, B. (eds), *A Tonic to the Nation. The Festival of Britain*, London, Thames and Hudson 1976.

Barclay, C. P., 'G. W. De Saulles, Engraver to the Mint', *The Medal*, no. 20. (Spring 1992).

Barnes, J., *Letters from London 1990-1995*, London, Picador 1995.

Beattie, S., *The New Sculpture*, New Haven and London, Yale University Press 1983.

Bielby, D., with Trusted, M., *British Sculpture 1470 to 2000. A concise catalogue of the collection at the Victoria & Albert Museum*, London, V&A Publications 2002.

Bignamini, I. and Hornsby, C., *Digging and Dealing in Eighteenth-century Rome*, 2 vols, New Haven and London, Yale University Press 2010.

Bindman, D. (ed.), *John Flaxman RA*, (exhibition catalogue) London, Royal Academy 1979.

Bindman, D. (ed.), *John Flaxman 1755-1826, Master of the Purist Line*, (exhibition catalogue) London, Sir John Soane's Museum and University College 2003.

Bindman, D., see Baker, M. 1995.

Black, J., 'The medal as political propaganda, a provincial example of 1739', *The Medal*, no. 10 (Winter 1986).

Borg. A., see Coke 2011.

Bradley, S. and Pevsner N., *London 1: City of London, Buildings of England*, New Haven and London, Yale University Press 1999.

Bradley, S. and Pevsner N., *London 6: Westminster, Buildings of England*, New Haven and London, Yale University Press 2003.

Brooke, C., and Cursi, V., *Hogarth Reynolds Turner, British Painting and the Rise of Modernity*, (exhibition catalogue) Rome, Fondazione Roma Museum 2014.

Bryant, J., *Thomas Banks 1735-1805 Britain's First Modern Sculptor*, (exhibition catalogue) London, Sir John Soane's Museum 2005.

Burnett, A. M., *Coins: Interpreting the Past*, London, British Museum Press 1991.

Byatt, D., *Promises to Pay: The First Three Hundred Years of Bank of England Notes*, London, Spink 1994.

Camden, W., variously titled *Britannia: A chorographical description of the most flourishing Kingdomes of England, Scotland and Ireland, and the Ilands adioyning, out of the depth of Antiquitie*, London 1586, 1607, and later editions.

Casey, P. J., *Roman Coinage in Britain*, Oxford, Shire Archaeology 1980 (rep. 2012).

Cavanagh, T., *Public Sculpture of the City of London*, Public Sculpture of Britain Series, Liverpool, Liverpool University Press in association with the Public Monuments and Sculpture Association 1997.

Challis, C. E. (ed.), *A New History of the Royal Mint*, Cambridge, Cambridge University Press 1992.

Chadwick, J., 'The Image of Britannia in Eighteenth Century Caricature', (unpublished MA thesis in the History of Art, Brookes University 2007).

Clancy, K., 'The British Trade Dollar', *Oriental Numismatic Newsletter*, no. 169 (Autumn 2001).

Clancy, K. (ed.) *Royal Mint Collector Coins, the story behind the 2007 collection*, Huddersfield, Jeremy Mills Publishing Ltd 2006.

Clancy, K. (ed.), *Designing Change: The Art of Coin Design*, Llantrisant, Royal Mint 2008.

Clancy, K., 'Receiving change: reaction to the new designs', in K. Clancy, (ed.), *Designing Change The Art of Coin Design*, Llantrisant, Royal Mint 2008.

Clancy, K., *A History of the Sovereign, Chief Coin of the World*, Llantrisant, Royal Mint Museum 2015.

Clarke, A. M., and Peters Bowron, E. (eds), *Pompeo Batoni. A Complete Catalogue of his Works with an Introductory Text*, Oxford, Oxford University Press 1985.

Clay, R. and Tungate, S. (eds), *Matthew Boulton and the Art of Making Money*, Studley, Brewin Books Ltd, 2009.

Cocke, R., *Public Sculpture of Norfolk and Suffolk*, Public Sculpture of Britain Series, Liverpool, Liverpool University Press in association with the Public Monuments and Sculpture Association 2013.

Coke, D., and Borg, A., *Vauxhall Gardens: A History*, New Haven and London, Yale University Press 2011.

Colley, L. *Britons Forging the Nation 1707-1837*, New Haven and London, Yale University Press 1992.

Colvin, H., *A Biographical Dictionary of British Architects 1600-1840*, New Haven and London, Yale University Press (3rd ed.) 1995.

Cook, B. (ed.), *The British Museum and the Future of UK Numismatics*, *Proceedings of a conference held to mark the 150th anniversary of the British Museum's Department of Coins and Medals*, London, British Museum Press 2011.

Cormack, L. B., 'Britannia Rules the Waves? Images of Empire in Elizabethan England', *Early Modern Literary Studies* (September 1998).

Cox, O., 'The Cult of Alfred', in S. Parissien, *Celebrating Britain, Canaletto, Hogarth and Patriotism*, London, Paul Holberton Publishing 2015.

Cox-Johnson A., *John Bacon RA 1740-99*, St Marylebone Society Publication no. 4, 1961.

Craig, J., *The Mint. A History of the London Mint, from AD 287 to 1948*, Cambridge University Press 1953.

Craske, M., *The Silent Rhetoric of the Body, A History of Monumnetal Sculpture abd Commemorative Art in England 1720-1770*, New Haven and London, Yale University Press 2007.

Crellin, S., *The Sculpture of Charles Wheeler*, London, Lund Humphries 2013.

Cronin, V., *A Pearl to India: The Life of Roberto de Nobili*, London, Rupert Hart-Davis 1959.

Crowley, J. E., *Imperial Landscapes. Britain's Global Visual Culture*, New Haven and London, Yale University Press 2011.

Cubitt, G. (ed.), *Imagining Nations*, Manchester, Manchester University Press 1998.

Curtis, P. (ed.), *Patronage & Practice Sculpture on Merseyside Liverpool*, Tate Gallery, Liverpool and National Museums on Merseyside 1989.

De Beer, E. S. (ed.), *The Diary of John Evelyn*, 6 vols, Oxford, Oxford University Press 1955.

Dobraszczyk, P., *Iron, Ornament and Architecture in Victorian Britain: Myth and Modernity*, Farnham, Ashgate 2014.

Dodd, D. see Jervis 2014.

Dyer, G. P., *The Proposed Coinage of King Edward VIII*, London, HMSO 1973.

Dyer, G. P. and Gaspar, P. P., 'Richard Sainthill and the new Bronze Coinage', *British Numismatic Journal*, vol. 54, 1984.

Dyer, G. P., *The Royal Mint, An Illustrated History*, Llantrisant, The Royal Mint 1986.

Dyer, G. P. and Gaspar, P. P., *The Standing Britannia Patterns of 1788*, paper to the British Numismatic Society, January 2004.

Eagleton, C., and Williams, J., *Money A History*, London, British Museum Press 1997 (rep. 2013).

Eagleton, C., 'Christopher Ironside and the designs for the decimal coinage', in K. Clancy (ed.), *Designing Change The Art of Coin Design*, Llantrisant, Royal Mint 2008.

Erim, K.T., 'A New Relief Showing Claudius and Britannia from Aphrodisias', *Britannia*, 13, 1982.

Eustace, K. (ed.), *Michael Rysbrack Sculptor 1694-1770*, (exhibition catalogue), Bristol City Museum and Art Gallery 1982.

Eustace, K., 'The Influence of the Antique on Sculpture in England 1560-1640', (unpublished MA dissertation, Courtauld Institute of Art, London 1985).

Eustace, K., 'Robert Adam, Charles-Louis Clérisseau, Michael Rysbrack and the Hopetoun chimneypiece', *Burlington Magazine*, CXXXIX, November 1997.

Eustace, K., 'The Post-Reformation Monuments', in P. Collinson, N. Ramsay, and M. Sparks (eds), *A History of Canterbury Cathedral*, Oxford, Oxford University Press 1995, (2nd ed. 2004).

Eustace, K. (ed.), *Canova Ideal Heads*, (exhibition catalogue) Oxford, Ashmolean Museum 1997.

Eustace, K., 'The Politics of the Past: Stowe and the development of the historical Portrait bust', *Apollo* CXLVIII, no.437 (July 1998).

Eustace, K., 'Britannia: the Woman on the Coin', *Fleur de Coin Review*, Issue 24, December 2005, Llantrisant, Royal Mint.

Eustace, K., 'Britannia: Some High Points in the History of the Iconography on British Coinage', *British Numismatic Journal*, 76, 2006.

Eustace, K., '"A Place full of rich and Industrious People": Art and patronage in Bristol in the first half of the 18th century', *British Art Journal*, VII no.1, (Spring/Summer 2006).

Eustace, K., 'The Key is Locke, Hogarth, Rysbrack and the Foundling Hospital', *British Art Journal*, VII no. 2, (Autumn 2006).

Eustace, K., 'Bread and Sermons: History in the Public Acknowledgment of Individual Lives', in F. W. Greenacre and D. Merritt (eds), *Public Sculpture of Bristol*, Public Sculpture of Britain Series, Liverpool, Liverpool University Press with the Public Monuments and Sculpture Association 2011.

Evelyn, J., Numismata, *A Discourse of Medals Antient and Modern Together with some accounts of Heads and Effigies of Illustrious and Famous Persons...*, London, Benjamin Tooke 1697.

Evelyn, J., *Diary*, see De Beer (ed.).

Flaxman, J., *A Letter to the Committee for raising the Naval Pillar or Monument, under the patronage of His Royal Highness The Duke of Clarence...*, London, T. Cadell & W. Davies 1779.

Flaxman, J., *Lectures on Sculpture*, London 1838 (Royal Academy Collections (07/4623)).

Forrer, L. S., *Le Type de "Britannia" sur les Monnais de la Grand Bretagne*, Macon, France 1907.

Forrer, L. S., *Biographical Dictionary of Medallists*, 8 vols, London, Spink and Son 1903-23.

Forrester, H., 'The Other Percy Metcalfe', *The Medal*, no. 49, 2006.

Foskett, D., *Samuel Cooper 1609-1672*, London, Faber and Faber 1974.

Frayling, C., 'Continuity through change: the Royal Mint Advisory Committee', in K. Clancy (ed.), *Designing Change, The Art of Coin Design*, Llantrisant, Royal Mint 2008.

Games, N., and Webb, B., *Abram Games Design*, Woodbridge, Antique Collectors' Club 2013.

Gardner, J., *The Artful Designer, Ideas off the drawing board*, London, Centurion Press 1993.

Gentleman, D., *Design in Miniature*, London, Studio Vista 1972.

Gentleman, D., 'Britannia and La Semeuse', *Fleur de Coin Review*, Issue 23, December 2004, Llantrisant, Royal Mint.

Girouard, M., *The Return to Camelot: Chivalry and the English Gentleman*, New Haven and London, Yale University Press 1981

Greenacre, F. W., *Marine Artists of Bristol: Nicholas Pocock and Joseph Walter*, (exhibition catalogue) Bristol, City of Bristol Museum and Art Gallery, 1982.

Greenacre, F. W., see Merritt 2011.

Guilding R., *Owning the Past Why the English Collected Antique Sculpture*, 1640-1840, New Haven and London, Yale University Press 2014.

Hamer, S. H., 'Notes on the private tokens, their issuers and die-sinkers', *British Numismatic Journal*, 1-3, 1904-6.

Hardy, E., see Roscoe 2009.

Harris, O. D., 'William Camden, Philemon Holland and the 1610 Translation of Britannia', *Antiquaries Journal*, vol. 95 2015.

Hart, V., *Inigo Jones, the Architect of Kings*, New Haven and London, Yale University Press 2011.

Haskell, F. and Penny, N., *Taste and the Antique, the Lure of Classical Sculpture 1500-1900*, New Haven and London, 1981.

Haslam, R., 'Concord Restored and Victory Assured', *Country Life* CXCI no. 34 (21 August 1997).

Hawksley, L., *The Mystery of Princess Louise, Queen Victoria's Rebellious Daughter*, London, Vintage Books 2014.

Hearn, K., 'Art in Britain Between 1530 & 1620', in S. Smiles (ed.), *West Country to World's End, the South-West in the Tudor Age* (exhibition catalogue), Royal Albert Memorial Museum & Art Gallery, Paul Hulberton Publishing 2014.

Hewitt, V. and Keyworth, J. M., *As Good as Gold: 300 Years of British Bank Note Design*, London, British Museum Publications 1987.

Hewitt, V., 'Britannia (fl. 1st-21st century)', *Oxford Dictionary of National Biography*, Oxford, Oxford University Press 2004.

Hewitt, V., *Beauty and the Bank: Images of Women on Paper Money*, London, British Museum Press 1994.

Howarth, D., *Lord Arundel and his Circle*, New Haven and London, Yale University Press 1985.

Ironside, J., 'Don't run up a Flag', *Fleur de Coin Review*, issue 12, February 1997, Llantrisant, Royal Mint.

Irwin, D., *John Flaxman 1755-1826, Sculptor, Illustrator, Designer*, London, Studio Vista 1979.

Jervis S. S., and Dodd D., *Roman Splendour English Arcadia, the English Taste for Pietre Dure and the Sixtus Cabinet at Stourhead*, National Trust, Philip Wilson Publishers, 2014.

Jones, M., *The Art of the Medal*, London, British Museum Publications Ltd. 1979.

Jones, M. (ed.), *Designs on Posterity: Drawings for Medals*, London, British Art Medal Trust 1979.

Jones S., *Frederick, Prince of Wales and his Circle*, (exhibition catalogue) Gainsborough's House, Sudbury 1981.

Keyworth, J. M., *Security by Design. A Closer Look at Bank of England Notes*, London, Bank of England Museum 2007.

Keyworth, J. M., see Hewitt 1987.

Latham, R. C. and Matthews, W., *The Diary of Samuel Pepys* (8 vols), London 1971.

Le Blanc, F., *Traité Historique des Monnoyes de France*, Paris, Pierre Mortier 1690, and Amsterdam 1692.

Lewis, J. E., *The English Fable: Aesop and Literary Culture, 1651-1740*, Cambridge, Cambridge University Press 1996.

Lindholm, R. C., 'Britannia: Symbol or Propaganda Device?', *Numismatist*, July 1994.

Longstaffe-Gowan T., 'Brazen proclamations: the deployment of statuary in some early London garden squares', *Sculpture Journal*, 18.1 (2009).

McDermott, C., *Masterpieces of Modern Design*, Hong Kong, Goodman Books and the Design Museum London 2013.

Macleod, C., see Marciari 2001.

Major, E., *Madam Britannia: Women, Church, and Nation 1712-1812*, Oxford, Oxford University Press 2012.

Marciari, A. J. and Macleod, C. (eds) *Painted Ladies, Women at the Court of Charles II*, (exhibition catalogue), London, National Portrait Gallery 2001.

Margoliouth, H. M. (ed.), *The Poems and Letters of Andrew Marvell*, I, Oxford, Oxford University Press, 1971.

Marsh, M. A., *Benedetto Pistrucci Principal Engraver and Chief Medallist of the Royal Mint*, Hardwick, Michael A. Marsh (Publications) 1996.

Marshall, P. J. (ed.), *The Eighteenth Century*, Oxford History of the British Empire, Oxford, Oxford University Press 1998 (2001).

Martin, E., 'Framing Victoria: royal portraiture and architectural sculpture in Victorian Britain', *Sculpture Journal*, February 2014.

Massie, J., *Observations Relating to the Coin of Britain, Consisting of Extracts from Mr Locke's Treatise concerning Money*, London 1760.

Merritt, D. and Greenacre, F. W., *Public Sculpture of Bristol*, Public Sculpture of Britain Series, Liverpool, Liverpool University Press in association with the Public Monuments and Sculpture Association 2011.

Mitchell, S., *Visions of Britain, 1730-1830, Anglo-Scottish Writing and Representation*, Basingstoke, Palgrave Macmillan 2013.

Mitter, P., *Much Maligned Monsters a History of European Reactions to Indian Art*, Oxford, Oxford University Press 1977.

Mitter, P., *Occidental Orientations: Art and Nationalism in Colonial India, 1850-1922*, Cambridge, Cambridge University Press 1994.

Mitter, P., *Indian Art*, Oxford, Oxford University Press 2001.

Moriarty, C. (ed.), *Abram Games: Maximum Meaning Minimum Means* (exhibition catalogue) London, Design Museum 2003.

Morrieson, H. W., 'A review of the Coinage of Charles II', *British Numismatic Journal* 15, (1919-20).

Murphy, P., *Nineteenth Century Irish Sculpture: native genius reaffirmed*, New Haven and London, Yale University Press 2010.

Myrone, M. (ed.), *Rude Britannia: British Comic Art*, London, Tate Publishing 2010.

Nathan, P., 'A British Britannia', in *The Britannia Gold Bullion Coin*, Llantrisant, Royal Mint 1987.

Norman, E., see White 2011.

Oliver, L., *Boris Anrep, The National Gallery Mosaics*, London, Yale University Press and National Gallery Company 2004.

Oman, C., *The Coinage of England*, Oxford, Oxford University Press 1931.

Orgal, S. and Strong, R., *Inigo Jones. The Theatre of the Stuart Court*, New York 1973.

Peacham, H., *Minerva Britanna Or A Garden Of Heroical Deuises, furnished, and adorned with Emblemes and Impresa's of sundry natures*, London, W. Dight 1612 (facsimile Da Capo Press, Amsterdam and New York 1971).

Peacham, H., *The Compleat Gentleman*, London 1622 (facsimile Da Capo Press, Amsterdam and New York 1968).

Peck, C. W., *English Copper, Tin and Bronze Coins in the British Museum 1558-1958*, London, British Museum 1960.

Penny, N., *Church Monuments in Romantic England*, New Haven and London, Yale University Press 1977.

Penny, N. see Haskell 1981.

Penny, N., *Catalogue of European Sculpture in the Ashmolean. 1540 to the Present Day*, Oxford, Oxford University Press, 1992, 3 vols.

Pepys, S., *Diary*, see Latham, R.C. and Matthews, W. (eds).

Peters Bowron, E. (ed.), *Pompeo Batoni (1708-87) and his British Patrons*, (exhibition catalogue) Iveagh Bequest Kenwood, Greater London Council 1982.

Peters Bowron, E. (ed.), see Clarke 1985.

Peters Bowron, E., and Kerber, P. B., *Pompeo Batoni, Prince of Painters in Eighteenth-century Rome*, New Haven and London, Yale University Press in association with the Museum of Fine Arts Houston 2007.

Phillips, T., *We Are the People: Postcards from the Collection of Tom Phillips* (exhibition catalogue) London, National Portrait Gallery 2004.

Physick, J., *Designs for English Sculpture 1680-1860*, London, Victoria & Albert Museum 1969.

Piggott, S., *William Stukeley, An Eighteenth-Century Antiquarian*, London, Thames and Hudson 1950 (rev. 1985).

Pointon, M., 'Money and Nationalism', in G. Cubitt (ed.), *Imagining Nations*, Manchester, Manchester University Press 1998.

Porteous, J., *Coins in History*, London, Putnam 1969.

Preussen, B. von, '"A wild kind of Imagination": eclecticism and excess in the English rococo designs of Thomas Johnson', in *Rococo Echo. Art History and Historiography* from Cochin to Coppola, Hyde, M. L. and Scott, K., Oxford, Oxford University Press 2014.

Ramaswamy, S., *The Goddess and the Nation, Mapping Mother India*, Durham and London, Duke University 2010.

Rayner, P. A., *English Silver Coinage from 1649*, London, Seaby 1992.

Read, B., *Victorian Sculpture*, New Haven and London, Yale University Press 1989.

Rendall, J., 'Tacitus engendered: Gothic feminism' and British histories, c.1750-1800', in G. Cubitt (ed.), *Imagining Nations*, Manchester, Manchester University Press 1998.

Rennie, P., *Festival of Britain Design 1951*, Woodbridge, Antique Collectors' Club 2007 (reprint 2008).

Roscoe, I., 'Peter Scheemakers', *Walpole Society*, LXI (1999).

Roscoe, I., Hardy, E., and Sullivan, G. M. (eds), A *Biographical Dictionary of Sculptors in Britain 1660-1851*, New Haven and London, Yale University Press 2009.

Ruding, R., *Annals of the Coinage of Great Britain and its Dependencies*, 3 vols, London 1840 (3rd edn.) (1st edn. 1799).

Sainthill, R., *An Olla Podrida or Scraps, Numismatic, Antiquarian and Literary*, 2 vols, London, Nichols and Son 1844 and 1853.

Saxl, F. and Wittkower, R., *British Art and the Mediterranean*, Oxford, Oxford University Press 1948.

Seaby, P., *The Story of British Coinage*, London, Seaby 1985.

Seidmann, G., 'Nathaniel Marchant, Gem-engraver, 1739-1816', *Walpole Society*, LIII (1987).

Smiles, S., *The Image of Antiquity, Ancient Britain and the Romantic Imagination*, New Haven and London, Yale University Press 1994.

Smiles, S. (ed.), *West Country to World's End, the South-West in the Tudor Age* (exhibition catalogue), Royal Albert Memorial Museum & Art Gallery, Paul Hulberton Publishing 2014.

Smith, A. (ed.), et al., *Artist and Empire. Facing Britan's Imperial Past*, (exhibition catalogue) London, Tate Britain 2015.

Snoddy, T., *Dictionary of Irish Artists, 20th Century*, Dublin, Merlin Publishing 2002 (2nd edn.).

Spalding, F., *The Tate A History*, London, Tate Gallery Publishing 1998.

Stamp, G., 'Architectural Sculpture in Liverpool', in Curtis, P. (ed.), *Patronage & Practice Sculpture on Merseyside Liverpool*, Tate Gallery, Liverpool and National Museums on Merseyside 1989.

Strong, R., *Britannia Triumphans: Inigo Jones, Rubens and Whitehall Palace*, London, Thames & Hudson, Walter Neurath Memorial Lectures 1981.

Strong, R., *Gloriana: The Portraits of Queen Elizabeth I*, London, Thames and Hudson 1987.

Strong, R., 'Britannia: the Design. Rule Britannia', in *The Britannia Gold Bullion Coin*, Llanstrisant, Royal Mint 1987.

Sullivan, G. M., see Roscoe 2009.

Syson, L., 'Alexander, Apelles and Lysippus in the Renaissance – Coins, Medals and Pictures', in B. Cook (ed.), *The British Museum and the Future of UK Numismatics* (conference proceedings), Trustees of the British Museum 2011.

Tacitus, 'Agricola', in *On Britain and Germany*, H. Mattingly (trans), London, Penguin Books 1948 (reprint 1967).

Tanner, L. E. E., *Recollections of a Westminster Antiquary*, London, John Baker 1969.

Thorn Drury, G. (ed.), *The Poems of Edmund Waller*, 2 vols., London, George Routledge & Sons Ltd. [1905],

Toynbee, J. M. C., 'Britannia on Roman Coins of the Second Century A.D.', *Journal of Roman Studies*, 14 (1924).

Toynbee, J. M. C., 'Further Notes on Britannia Coin-Types', *Journal of Roman Studies*, 15 (1925).

Toynbee, J. M. C., *The Hadrianic School: A Chapter in the History of Greek Art*, Cambridge, Cambridge University Press 1934.

Trusted, M., see Bielby 2002.

Tungate, S., see Clay 2009.

Usher, R., *Protestant Dublin, 1660-1760*, Architecture and Iconography, Basingstoke, Palgrave Macmillan 2012.

Vertue, G., Notebooks I-VI, *Walpole Society*, XVIII, XX, XXII, XXIV, XXVI, XXX; Index XXIX. Oxford, Oxford University Press 1930-1952 (reprint 1968).

Wagner, G., *Thomas Coram, Gent. 1668-1751*, Woodbridge, Boydell Press 2004.

Ward-Jackson, P., *Public Sculpture of the City of London*, Public Sculpture of Britain Series, Liverpool, Liverpool University Press in association with the Public Monuments and Sculpture Association 2003.

Ward-Jackson, P., *Public Sculpture of Historic Westminster*, vol. I, Public Sculpture of Britain Series, Liverpool, Liverpool University Press in association with the Public Monuments and Sculpture Association 2011.

Warner, M., *Monuments and Maidens: The Allegory of the Female Form*, London, Weidenfeld and Nicholson 1985.

Whinney, M., *Sculpture in Britain 1530-1839*, Harmondsworth, Penguin Books Ltd. 1964.

White, A., 'A Biographical Dictionary of London Tomb Sculptors, *c*. 1560 - *c*. 1660', *Walpole Society*, LXI (1999).

White, D. and Norman, E., *The Public Sculpture of Sheffield and South Yorkshire*, Public Sculpture of Britain Series vol. 12, Liverpool, Liverpool University Press in association with the Public Monuments and Sculpture Association 2011.

Whitley, J., 'Drawings by the Master of the "Médaillons historiques"', *Master Drawings*, XXX (1992).

Whiteley, J., *French Ornament Drawings of the Sixteenth Century*, VI, Oxford, Clarendon Press 1996.

Whitlock Blundell, J., *Westminster Abbey, The Monuments*, London, John Murray 1989.

Wittkower, R., see Saxl 1948.

Wyon, A., *The Great Seals of England*, London, Chiswick Press 1887.

Yates, F. A., *Astraea: the Imperial Theme in the Sixteenth Century*, London, Routledge & Keegan Paul 1975 (reprint 1985).

Acknowledgements

When it was suggested that Sir Roy Strong should write the Foreword to this book, he immediately became the first person to thank, not just for his agreeing to write it, but because long ago he made it possible for me to remain at the Victoria & Albert Museum when the first cold winds of change began to blow at the museum. It was for him that I and my fellow Museums Association Student, Dr Elizabeth Darby, worked on the popularising exhibition *A Tonic to the Nation*, celebrating the very 50 years of progress in the political, social and artistic culture of our country that was even then drawing to a close. I owe in large measure my professional career of over 35 years in museums in this country to him.

Next to be thanked is my Editor, Kevin Clancy, who invited me to give a paper on the subject to the British Numismatic Society in 2004, encouraged me to publish it, and had enough faith in the outcome to commission this book. He and his team at the Royal Mint Museum, Claire Hughes, Abigail Kenvyn, Sarah Tyley and Chris Barker, have done everything to ensure the production was up to speed. I am grateful to them all, and to Nigel Tudman and his team at Tuch Design, Sukey Bhamra in particular, for bringing the book and its disparate parts together in this clean, contemporary design.

I owe a great debt to the distinguished numismatists Philip Attwood, Andrew Burnett, Graham Dyer, Sir Mark Jones, and Robin (John) Porteous, who all encouraged me and put me right in the kindest and most helpful of ways. In making searches many others have helped me, among them Sam Moorhead and the staff of the Department of Coins and Medals at the British Museum; in the Ashmolean Museum, Oxford, to Volker Heuchert I am grateful for valuable discussions, illustrations, and the generosity of shared knowledge, and Shailendra Bhandare, who gave me time, lent me books and set me on a path through the wood I had not expected to find. I am grateful also for the hospitality of the Heberden Coin Room in the Ashmolean, and from colleagues there present and past: Roz Britton-Strong, Nicholas Mayhew, Chris Howgego, and Henry Kim. Caroline Palmer and colleagues in the Print Room of the Ashmolean Museum; Juliet Chadwick, Colin Harris and Sarah Wheale in the Weston Library, the Bodleian Library, Oxford; and Graham Salmon at the Queen's College. At the Bank of England Rachel Muir and Eleanor Paton in the Archive, and Anna Spender and Helena Liszka in the Museum were immensely helpful, as was Ceri Brough in the National Gallery Archives.

Others to thank include Michael and Caroline Baker, Jill Combermere, Peter Howell, Michael Keene, Lucy May Maxwell, Fiona Pearson, David Symons, Robert Wenley, Bryan Ward Perkins, Philip Ward-Jackson and Arnold Wilson. At home James Hamilton and Marie Hamilton, who played Britannia in Kate O'Connor's production of Ed Musthill's *1912* in Dalston in 2014, now know as much about the subject as I do.